CRISIS

CRUCIBLE

OF PRAISE

Other books by Latayne C. Scott:

Fiction:

Latter-day Cipher

What Will Be Made Plain

The Mona Lisa Mirror Mystery

A Conspiracy of Breath

The Dream Quilt (under pen name Celeste Ryan)

Non-Fiction:

The Mormon Mirage: A Former Member Looks at the Mormon Church Today (3rd edition)

Why We Left Mormonism: Eight People Tell Their Stories (formerly titled, *Ex-Mormons: Why We Left*)

Why We Left a Cult: Six People Tell Their Stories

After Mormonism, What? Reclaiming the Ex-Mormon's Worldview for Christ

Time, Talents, Things: Studies in Biblical Stewardship

The Parables of Jesus

Just You, Me and God: A Devotional Guide for Couples Reading through the Bible in One Year

The Heart's Door: Hospitality in the Bible

Passion, Power, Proxy, Release: Communion Meditations

The Hinge of Your History: The Phases of Faith

The Red Cord of Hope: When History Stopped for One Woman of Faith

The Shout of the Bridegroom: Understanding Christ's Intimate Love for His Church (formerly titled *A Marriage Made in Heaven*, with R. Glenn Greenwood)

Open Up Your Life: A Women's Workshop in Christian Hospitality

To Love Each Other: A Women's Workshop on I Corinthians 13

Protecting Your Child from Predators: How to Recognize and Respond to Sexual Danger (with Dr. Beth Robinson)

Discovering the City of Sodom: The Fascinating, True Account of the Old Testament's Most Infamous City (with Steven Collins)

Leaving Mormonism: Why Four Scholars Changed their Minds (with Corey Miller, Lynn K. Wilder, and Vince Eccles)

Mountains of Mercy: One Family's Story of Hope in Crisis (with Lavone D. Genzink)

Novel Tips on Rice: What to Cook When You'd Rather Be Writing (with Bonnie Grove, Patti Hill, Kathleen Popa, Sharon K. Souza and Debbie Fuller Thomas)

CRISIS
CRUCIBLE
OF PRAISE

Finding Grace in the Midst of Adversity

LATAYNE C. SCOTT

TRINITY SOUTHWEST UNIVERSITY PRESS
Albuquerque, New Mexico

Trinity Southwest University Press
Albuquerque, New Mexico, USA

CRISIS CRUCIBLE OF PRAISE: Finding Grace in the Midst of
Adversity
Copyright @ 2020 by Latayne C. Scott

ISBN: 978-1945750120

Printed in the United States of America

Cover design by: Kimberly Eichel

With praise to God for that which in our lives has brought with it its own traditions: a history satisfying to recount; a storehouse of memories that together as a sum mean providence, protection, and a reason for hope in the future.

I acknowledge the great influence that three writers—C. S. Lewis, Philip Yancey, and Tim Stafford—and three readers—Margaret Talbot, Paula Huguley, and my editor, Bob Hudson—had on this manuscript.

I also gratefully acknowledge the patronage of Gary and Marie Smith, who made this new edition possible, and the editing of Sharon K. Souza, who made it readable.

This book is in the present tense of its original date of publication (1989.) I have only made minor changes so as not to confuse present-day readers by the chronology. It reflects how I felt then, raw from a season of great crisis. Now, of course, I am in a new decade of a different kind of crisis, but what I learned and concretized in this book was the foundation I stood on to weather new storms. May it bolster you against the winds of your life.

Contents

Introduction: Beginning to See

When I was eleven, something happened that changed my life. I got my first pair of eyeglasses.

Every year since I had begun school, I brought home little notices from the school nurse that said, "Have your child's eyes professionally examined." At first, due to tight family finances and frequent moves, my parents put off taking me to the eye doctor. Later, my father flatly and repeatedly refused. He thought I just wanted glasses to be like some of my friends who had them. The idea seemed to have great validity in his mind, especially since the school examinations indicated in the early grades that my situation was serious but later on showed my vision to be better.

That was, until that fateful day in the fifth grade on which the school nurse brought a new eye chart—one that did not have the large letter E at the end—one that I did not have time to memorize. That was the day I stood alone and humiliated before my classmates, one hand cupped over each eye in turn, tearfully whispering to the nurse, who proceeded line by line to the large black blur at the bottom of the chart, "I can't see."

Fifth-graders aren't kind. It was a disaster, one I had carefully staved off for five years by bathroom trips that put me at the back of lines so I could listen to and memorize the repeated litany of alphabet letters. My day of reckoning had arrived. I was teased unmercifully by some of my classmates who found in me a new victim who could be humbled by "Hey, blindy, how many fingers am I holding up?" Even my friends greeted this revelation with openmouthed, amazed looks and that stunned silence we use around the handicapped. That is, those who were within ten or so feet did—anyone any further away wore a blurred pink mask that obscured any facial expression.

Two weeks later I rode home in silence from the eye doctor's office, wearing a pair of pale blue cat-eye glasses. I remember that spring day and my astonishment at the world around me. Craning my neck, I looked out the side and front windows of the car and up at the sky. Suddenly I blurted out, "Mother, look at the leaves on the trees! All of them!"

Of course I knew that trees had leaves. I had climbed them, swung from their branches, torn spidery shapes from cottonwood leaves. Those trees had leaves. But as soon as I walked away from them, they became undulant, borderless green ghosts. Now, with my new eyeglasses, the two images merged.

I looked away. The hot, embarrassed silence that filled the car was almost palpable. I suppose it lasted the entire trip home, but I don't remember anything but my fascination at the miracle of leaves on every tree we passed that lovely spring day.

Many things changed. My grades improved—especially in those subjects like classroom music (which was taught on closed-circuit television) and math (taught on the blackboard). My posture improved, for now as I walked outside I could see things of more interest than the large rocks beneath my feet. Even my beloved reading of books became more pleasurable.

But to this day I remember my shame at being found out; my game of pretending had been exposed.

Oh, we know this game well, don't we? It is not just as children that we stare blankly at shapes in the clouds pointed out by others and say, "Yes, I see."

We tell ourselves it is for survival that we give up after years of trying to understand things and settle for memorizing facts to placate the questions of those around us. We do it to get by, but we are not proud of it. Sometimes we are even put in the position of having to teach those facts to others, and we do it, not because we know those facts, but because others seem to see them, and we know we should too. But we can't.

Then come the feelings of guilt, lack of genuineness, and hurt. Worst of all we withdraw from those who heard us proclaim those facts. We know they see them because they are so joyful, and we memorize more and more, and still we don't see.

Of course, we are no longer speaking of eye charts, nor of shapes in clouds, nor even of philosophical concepts passed from person to person. We are speaking of knowing God.

For each of us there are days of reckoning. I am not speaking of that final day of judgment before His throne—although that day is coming—but of those days when we are ripped apart and devoured by experiences beyond our control, experiences we call crises. They are days of reckoning because in them we test what we know, or think we know, about God.

Perhaps you are reading this book because you or someone close to you is involved in a crisis. If you are not at this moment facing a crisis, be assured of this: you will. Even if the only crisis you face in your life is your own death, it is coming.

At such times, we first use whatever resources we have to try to survive or to help someone else to survive. Only after this immediate need is addressed do we begin the inevitable second stage—to ask why. I am writing this book to meet those two needs: survival of the body and the soul.

There are no pat answers to fit every situation. In personal dilemmas we find that we are brothers and sisters to Job, who after asking all his questions found in God what he really needed—not answers to his questions about his life, but contact with the Answer to his life.

It is natural, our desperate seeking for explanations. After reflection most of us would admit we prefer knowing about God to knowing about ourselves. Self-knowledge is undeniably useful but limited in its applications when we are dealing with circumstances beyond our control. There are, however, discoveries we all make that help us understand ourselves and God much better, discoveries that we human beings can share with each other: lights in this great tunnel where we all reside.

For many years my Christian life was an active one of service to others. Except for my writing, I spent very little time in the "inner disciplines" of prayer and meditation. Oh, I "said my prayers," but I felt little emotional connection to the One to whom I was praying, for in many ways I kept Him at arm's length.

At one point, however, this disparity began to torment me. After months of emptiness my anguish culminated in my asking this distant God to break me, to use me in any way He wanted, kill me if necessary. Anything to really know Him.

And I do know Him. And the price has been worth it. Knowing Him has given me the strength to survive and to some extent understand certain situations in my life that were in the crisis category. I believe that what has made the difference is a true, biblical knowledge of what praising Him is and a rich, satisfying prayer life.

"Just praise the Lord and keep praying?" you might incredulously ask. Indeed, to someone deeply involved in a crisis, these words are often hatefully trite, the after-church proverbs of women with their minds on their too-done roasts in the oven, the surface Christian's equivalent of "don't call me, I'll call you."

But the letters on the eye chart are no less correct, no less true, when they are recited by those who do not see them; and the shallowness of our understanding can never negate God's truth. "Praise the Lord" is a phrase that by overuse has lost, for many of us, its real meaning, but being able to praise God—especially in crisis—is a rock-bottom, absolute necessity.

I have read every book I can get my hands on that deals with the subject of praise. There are several fine books on the market. But through reading those passages in the Bible that are praise passages, I have developed a definition of biblical praise that I think is not only more complete than those I've read, but also more helpful, especially to people in difficult situations.

Biblical praise (we'll look at specific examples later) seems to have three essential elements. The first is an acknowledgment of who God is. He is good, we sometimes blithely assume. But our human minds have the capacity to create gods who are not good: the Hindu goddess Kali, for instance, is bloodthirsty and vengeful. Or we create a "christian" god in our own image: indecisive, ambivalent, impotent, and unlovely. This, unfortunately, is the God we are wont to approach in times of crisis, when all divine help seems far away. Bible praise passages, in contrast, always identify the true God with attributes that are unmistakably divine and appealing.

They are all variations on the flatly-stated praise-facts of Psalm 62:1-12: "You, O God, are strong," and "You, O Lord, are loving." It is knowing that His power is greater than our own that drives us to Him, and it is our need for His love that keeps us there.

The second element of praise, that is, acknowledging what God has done, is illustrated by the Old Testament custom of reciting His wondrous deeds of the past. The Red Sea experience, for instance, has been used as a vehicle of praise for hundreds of years after it happened. The wonder of that event, and how it showed God's strength and love for His people, was still a living fact for Stephen, who died just moments after retelling the story.

Recalling God's workings inevitably leads to the conclusion that if He could do such things in the past, then, surely, He can work in the same way in the present. That is the third part of biblical praise.

This three-part definition of praise—acknowledging who God is, what He has done in the past, and concluding what He can do in the present—is an obvious and repeated pattern. We see it over and over in the Psalms, in the magnificats of Hannah and Mary, in Solomon's temple dedication prayer, in the chantings of the elders and four living creatures of the Revelation.

But it is, after all, only a pattern. Like the tissue-paper pieces we use to cut out fabric for our clothing, it shows us what to do but won't wear long in everyday life. Like the inherited faith of our parents, it is a story we often know about but do not *know*.

When, however, we begin to assess our own history with God, we too can say what we ourselves know to be true about Him. We can look back on times of happiness and fulfillment, and say with certainty, "He is a good God; He has always taken care of my needs." Continuing this assessment, we can itemize times when we were certain that He spared our lives, blessed those we love, gave us undeserved favors.

When we put this personal history together with that of the hundreds of witnesses in the Bible who affirm the same things about Him, we feel the assurance that we have rightly judged Him; and then the final step should be easy.

It should be, but it isn't. There seem to be two breaking points of faith when a Christian faces crisis. The first comes when we test what we know about God—His goodness and power—against the rottenness and impotence we are feeling. Even if we give mental assent to the fact that He is a good, caring God and that He has done great things in the past, it is sometimes an entirely different matter to face the second breaking point: that of knowing how to interpret what He is doing and will do about our particular situation in the present.

It is at that juncture, I believe, that our communication with God often breaks down. Many Christians—good, loving people—feel mistrustful, battered, sometimes even misused by the God whom they assume is allowing all these traumatic things to happen. We give Him "the silent treatment." We hurt and hurt, numbed and alone. We may feel we have been burned by what Willard Sperry called "the dangerous life of the Spirit." The singeing intimacy with God, the increased burden of confidentiality, the pain of contact; all may seem too much to bear.

I know, I've been there. I've felt these things. But God has manifested His power and His love in my life and has made these two facts about Himself—He is strong, and He is loving—the basis for my own hope for the future.

Between the time I asked God to break me and the crises I experienced, which I will tell you about later, He gave me time to prepare, to build the relationship with Him that was essential to my spiritual survival. Yes, I had survived other earlier crises in my life without this closeness to Him, but He knew these coming times would be different. There were some things I needed to know.

"What if I don't have that time?" you ask.

The fact that you are reading means that He is giving you the time to prepare right now.

PART ONE

Principles of Praise

THE MEASURE OF THINGS

I am proving
The substance of eternity

I test its elasticity
With searching hands
(I find I am caught in a bubble
Just on its outer rim)

Like a scientist
I log its reaction
To different stimuli:
Prayer warms it,
Doubt constricts it;
It recoils distastefully
From despair

Why does all the data
Hurt so?

Only in
You,
The ultimate experiment of faith,
Does anything
Make any sense

ONE

A Crisis Begins

"Mom, my head hurts."

My blond-headed daughter staggered, melodramatically I thought, across the ceramic-tile entryway of our Boulder, Colorado, home. She tossed her backpack full of schoolbooks, papers, and stuffed toys onto the stairway and heaved her sturdy form onto the third step beside me— this was our tradition. I always tried to meet her at the door when she came home from school to look over her papers and discuss the day she'd had.

I took her in my arms. It had been hard, I knew, moving our two children here after they'd lived all their short lives in Albuquerque. But as I'd promised, God had provided new friends and new experiences. Ryan, our rambunctious and self-assured nine-year-old, had fallen right into the groove of soccer and boys' stuff. But Celeste, gentle, sensitive Celeste, had taken to the adjustment period more reluctantly. This, combined with her frustration with her stocky frame in a thin-kid world, sometimes made her feel sorry for herself.

I reached for the part of her head she pointed to, but she recoiled. "Would you like an aspirin?" I asked, soothing her. She shook her head. I felt under her jaws to check for gland swelling—her frequent bouts with strep often began with a headache. I found nothing.

The coming days brought uncharacteristic temper tantrums from her, which I attributed to the excitement of planning her eighth birthday party. Also, my husband, Dan, and I were contemplating not only another move, but a complete change of career for him. Over and over I had prayed that God would give us an obvious sign of His will.

At any rate, several days passed with Celeste attributing all her woes to a headache and me thinking that it was just her way of getting some much-needed attention. But as I put her to bed one night later that week, I noticed tears on her cheeks.

"Mom, my head still hurts," she sobbed.

"Did you bump it at school? Did anyone accidentally hit you? Have you been under a table or desk and come up suddenly?" All my queries met with no success. Again I tried to touch the part of her head she pointed to. Again she recoiled, crying. Against her screaming refusals I parted the hair at the back of her head and discovered the culprit: a smooth, firm, nickel-sized lump that seemed to be just under the surface of the skin. It was obvious that even the slightest pressure caused Celeste great pain. But it wasn't bruised; in fact it was the same pale pink as the rest of her scalp.

The next morning I called her pediatrician, Dr. Gehres, who thought, as I had, that it was perhaps just a "goose egg" from a forgotten minor injury. "Wait a few days," she said, "and if it's not smaller, bring her in."

The lump did not subside. "It's hard to tell what it could be," Dr. Gehres mused in her office later that week, "but I'd be willing to bet it's just an oil gland that got plugged up and formed a sebaceous cyst. We'll get her right on an antibiotic." I left her office feeling a little like an overprotective mom but somewhat paradoxically comforted by the fact that the doctor was not too concerned. Celeste started taking the antibiotics, and each morning I would gently part her hair and look at the smooth unyielding surface of the lump.

By Sunday, halfway through her round of antibiotics, I knew something was wrong. The feeling was a familiar one. In 1978, when she was five months old, she contracted one of the virulent strains of Asian flu. I spent an entire weekend phoning the doctor on call (her regular pediatrician was on vacation) and telling him that my baby didn't look right. He kept asking (with increasing irritation) what her temperature and symptoms were. Neither seemed serious to him, but after the fifth call I insisted that he see Celeste. He met me at a hospital emergency room and within five minutes admitted her to the hospital—with pneumonia—where she spent the next eight days under an oxygen tent, hanging on to her young life.

I learned two important lessons from that experience. One was that if a mother thinks her child is ill, she should have the child examined by a doctor no matter what anyone else says. The other thing I inferred from this was that such intuition is not just from myself—the Holy Spirit surely had a part in it.

Now I faced that same feeling. During communion that morning at the Church of Christ we attended, I stared at the raised area at the front of the auditorium and a terrifying image flashed through my mind. I could see there, in my mind's eye, a small casket. No matter how much I reassured myself that I was just acting out a "worst-case scenario," I still could not fight back the tears. "No, Lord, don't let her die," I prayed. "Not Celeste."

We returned home and I prepared lunch, hiding my distress from my family. Celeste had gone to spend the afternoon with a friend, and Ryan and my husband, Dan, went downstairs to watch a football game. I went to the bedroom, my praying place, and began to pour out my heart to God. I was so afraid, so helpless. There, in the shadows of that October afternoon, I begged God for the life of my child.

Later that afternoon I called my dear friend Molly Harvey in Albuquerque and confided my fears to her. As far as I could tell, the lump had actually increased in size over the past few days. I hadn't told anyone of my terrible feeling— not even my husband, who was wrestling with those important career decisions. Molly promised to pray for us, and I resolved to call the doctor again in the morning.

Dr. Gehres was gentle and encouraging. "It does surprise me that the lump hasn't responded," she said. "Why don't you see a dermatologist?"

I called and made an immediate appointment with a local specialist, Dr. Russell. When Celeste came home from school, our "stairway talk" was about more than school. Having undergone several painful experiences with doctors, she was wary of anyone in a white jacket. She wanted to know exactly what he would do to her. The appointment secretary had mentioned the possibility of a biopsy; so I tried as honestly and as delicately as I could to describe what that might be like. Characteristically, Celeste was not satisfied until I had described everything I thought he might possibly do. There, on the stairs, we prayed for Dr. Russell and the lump.

After praying with Celeste that night at bedtime, I lingered at her door, looking at her and noting how she slept on her side—the lump made it too painful for her to assume her usual posture on her back. I was filled with anger and resentment at that protruding mass on her head. By now it was the size of half of a golf ball. I felt an urge to get a large needle and lance it while she slept, to rid her of this implacable, silent enemy of her health and my peace of mind. I wanted to see what was inside, what was causing all this. With a gasp, I realized how foolish such an action would be—not only to her health, but also to my peace of mind. I was jarred by the realization that this lump was just a visible symbol of sin. No, the lump was not the result of some dark sins in Celeste's life. But sin itself was what brought death into the world—and sickness and hurting and lumps on the head, like hers. I tried to direct my anger where it should go—at Satan, that old deceiver, that author of sin. At that moment, I hated him more than I have ever hated anyone or anything in my life.

When we went to Dr. Russell's office the next day, I immediately felt good about my choice of a dermatologist— not only because he agreed to see Celeste so quickly, but also because his office was filled with photographs of his own blond-headed children. He had a daughter just Celeste's age, and he was adept at soothing the fears of our child—and ourselves. As he smoothed away her hair, he saw Dan's and my tense postures and tried to help us relax.

"I'm almost positive this is just a fatty tumor," he reassured us. Dan immediately brightened.

"My grandfather had one of those," he remembered. "In fact, he had it for several years, and it never hurt him."

"That's right," said Dr. Russell. "Only if they become uncomfortable, say, rubbing against clothing, is it necessary to remove them." He smiled at Celeste.

The nagging feeling was still there with me. "But how can you be sure?" I questioned. "I mean, how can you know that it is a fatty tumor?"

"Well, that would take a biopsy."

"So let's do one." I heard my voice say these words with a pushy quality I didn't like.

Both the doctor and Dan looked at me with faint surprise. Apologetically, I added, "It seems like whenever anyone in our family has a hangnail, we end up with an amputated foot."

My exaggerated statement really wasn't completely untrue. In 1970 Dan had broken his leg while playing baseball, and while the two bones were being set, he developed a pulmonary embolism that put him into a coma. After recovering from that, a stomachache three years later turned out to be a symptom of a lodged kidney stone that required a complicated surgical procedure his urologist characterized as having a lower success rate than a kidney transplant. When I went into labor with Ryan, a simple delivery turned into an emergency cesarean section where Ryan was born "severely depressed," medically speaking, and was not out of danger for several days. I developed an infection that kept me hospitalized for eleven days.

Even Dan's routine vasectomy after my C-section delivery of Celeste didn't "take" and, much to his chagrin, had to be repeated. As a family we really had no reason to expect the ordinary out of any medical procedure.

Dr. Russell listened, smiling. "Don't worry. This is not cancer or anything like that," he reassured. "But we'll schedule a biopsy anyway."

"Why not do it now?" I asked.

"Well, we'd have to prepare Celeste." His voice trailed off.

I drew her close to me. "Dr. Russell, she and I have discussed what a biopsy's like, and we've prayed about it. We're ready any time you are. We're ready right now."

He looked searchingly at Celeste, and she met his eyes with an unblinking gaze of trust. He called in a nurse to bring the materials to deaden her scalp and perform the biopsy. As he described what he was going to do, Celeste nodded serenely. He patted the examination table, and she unhesitatingly hoisted herself up onto it and lay face down, her hands tucked under her thighs.

No screams, no protests. Dr. Russell and his nurse looked at each other in amazement. Only when the stinging needle full of anesthetic pierced her skin did fat teardrops fall silently onto the table. My resolution to watch the procedure fled when I saw the first drops of blood under his scalpel. Dan and I huddled in chairs, eyes averted, in the silence of the room.

AFTER THE BIOPSY AND SKULL X-RAYS

What demon has taken my daughter
Clutching at her from inside outside
With talons called tumors

As the blood yet oozes from sutures
She stares in backward fascination
With a tiny handheld mirror

Then there are the inevitable phone calls.
I recite the catechism of pain.
I blunt their concern with
A stiffening shield of hope:

I am either a fool, or . . .

Were it someone else's child
I would let myself feel the pain more
Intensely—I would visualize
The horror that I erase
Each time the automatic
Blackboard of mind begins
To write

TWO

A Crisis Concludes

"Just fat cells?"

I had called his office three times to get the results of the biopsy that the lab had delayed, and now that I had the results, I just couldn't believe my ears. Sure, my Tuesday morning Bible class that met in our home had prayed for good results on this test, and knew I should be grateful that the lump seemed to be so innocuous, only a fatty tumor. "You don't have to be in a hurry to remove this lump," said Dr. Russell. "You can let the biopsy scar heal and—"

I interrupted him. "Please—let's remove it right away." When Ryan and Celeste returned from school and Dan returned from work, I had accomplished a lot. The removal of the lump was scheduled for that Friday, the procedure to be done, again under local anesthetic, in Dr. Russell's office. I had called my Bible-class members and asked them for further prayers, then telephoned my best friend, my beloved prayer partner, and asked for the special support only that one person could give. I felt spiritually prepared for what I knew in my heart of hearts was going to be a difficult experience because I felt the strength of those prayers already ascending to God.

Also growing in my heart was an increasing resolution to make this a time when I could confirm to God my love for Him and my trust in Him. I promised Him verbally, over and over, that I would trust Him with Celeste's health.

My mother flew out from Albuquerque, her long-planned trip coinciding (not accidentally, I knew, but in God's plan) with the Friday office visit. Dan, Celeste, and I left right after school that day while

Mother stayed with Ryan. Again, Celeste laid herself down on the table without a word while Dr. Russell, chatting soothingly, began to cut away the growth.

After a few minutes his smile faded. He no longer spoke. He was grim after he finished the procedure. As we hugged Celeste and congratulated her on her bravery, he pulled a chair up to ours.

"Has Celeste ever had a skull X-ray?"

Our short-lived relief vanished. Dan and I looked at each other, mute, as we shook our heads.

"I want you to take her right now across the street to Community Hospital. I'll call ahead and schedule the X-ray." He continued as we looked astonished at him. "You see, as I began to remove the lump, I discovered there is no bone underneath it." His face paled visibly as he looked at Celeste. "I'm just glad I didn't scrape where the bone should have been—I would have gone into her brain."

Dan and I walked woodenly over to the hospital with the unreal, puppet-like motions we humans feel when any tragedy overtakes us. Celeste seemed oblivious to our stunned grief—she knew X-rays didn't hurt and knew she was over the worst. The radiologist confirmed Dr. Russell's findings: there was no bone where the lump had been, and until the tumor tissue was analyzed, there could be no firm diagnosis.

There in the waiting room, Dan grasped Dr. Russell's arm firmly. "If she were your daughter," he asked, "what would you do?"

Dr. Russell seemed relieved that we were not angry with him. He turned his attention to the future. "I'd consult the best neurosurgeon I could find," he said. "Dr. Richard Pressley. I'll get in touch with him, have him go over the X-rays, and have him call you at home tonight."

We walked out into the parking lot just as the sun was setting. Dan had come straight from work in his own car and whispered to me in a tear-choked voice that he needed some time alone. I knew Mother would be worried because we had been gone so long, so I told him I would go straight home and wait for him. He drove off, his shoulders shaking.

As the anesthetic began to wear off during the ride home, Celeste's awareness of something wrong heightened. I explained to her what I understood of her condition, and she listened gravely and then joined me as we reassured each other of God's control of this situation.

By the time Dan arrived home an hour later, had repeated the afternoon's events over and over to Mother and Ryan, to Dan's mother who'd called long distance, to members of my Tuesday-morning and Wednesday-night classes where I'd requested prayers, to friends from New Mexico and Texas. Soon Dr. Pressley called with his diagnosis: he felt sure that the growth was an eosinophilic granuloma, a rare tumor that originated inside the bone and destroyed that bone as it grew.

Sunday morning was an emotional time as Dan and I described in a written note to the congregation Celeste's condition and our pain. We requested prayers and received an outpouring of love from our brothers and sisters. Only later did I realize the meaning of a special hug from the wife of one of our elders—her son had lost his leg to another type of granuloma just seven years before.

As Dan and the children took Mother to the airport later that afternoon, I had a chance to be alone with God. I thanked Him that the fear at last had a name—an enemy that could be fought (if not pronounced). I praised Him for preventing Dr. Russell from the scraping that was so routine in the removal of a fatty tumor. I didn't know how this tumor could be treated—but I did know the Creator of Celeste's body—and He knew what to do.

How unlike the Sunday before when I had wept in fear! A Bible passage came to mind and I read it over and over:

> Brothers, we do not want you to be ignorant about
> those who fall asleep, or to grieve like the rest of men,

who have no hope. We believe that Jesus died and rose
again and so we believe that God will bring with Jesus
those who have fallen asleep in him. According to the
Lord's own word, we tell you that we who are still alive,
who are left till the coming of the Lord, will certainly not
precede those who have fallen asleep. For the Lord
himself will come down from heaven, with a loud
command, with the voice of the archangel and with the
trumpet call of God, and the dead in Christ will rise first.
After that, we who are still alive and are left will be caught
up together with them in the clouds to meet the Lord in
the air. And so we will be with the Lord forever.
Therefore encourage each other with these words.

1 Thessalonians 4:13-18

And these words did encourage me! Though the situation outwardly
looked much more bleak than last week, I was filled with praise for the
God of our lives. Instead of begging Him for her life, I willingly—
verbally—gave Him permission to do whatever He saw fit with her,
knowing that He must love her even more than I could. And then I spent
the rest of the afternoon lying on my bed, singing through a sob-
thickened throat every praise song I knew.

. After Celeste went to bed that night, Ryan demanded a conference
with us, and I realized with an ache how our attentions of the past week
had overlooked him. But now he wanted some answers. He wasted no
time in coming to the point.

"Is Celeste . . ." His voice quivered. "Is she going to, um, die? "

Dan was overcome with emotion, his unspoken fears verbalized by
our young son. We both hugged Ryan and told him how much we loved
and appreciated his concern for Celeste and his helpful attitude of the
past weeks. We all cried as I spoke.

"Ryan, son, I don't know if she's going to die. We don't want her to, because we love her just like we love you. But we do know that God's in control of this situation. We are trusting Him to do the best thing.

"But we also know that dying is not the worst thing that can happen to a Christian. Celeste loves the Lord, and if she dies, she'll go to heaven to be with Him. And you know what? If she dies, I'll be jealous!"

His eyes opened wide. "Why, Mom?"

"Because she'll be there before me. Heaven is where I want to go too."

I could feel him relaxing in my arms. Death can't have a sting for the Christian who is not afraid of it.

At Dr. Pressley's office on Tuesday, he outlined several courses of action to treat the growing tumor. Radiation, chemotherapy, and steroids were all possibilities, but we agreed that immediate surgery to cut away the edges of the diseased bone was the quickest and most effective. He stressed that only surgery could reveal whether the tumor had damaged the brain, and he read to us a long list of possible—though unlikely—side effects of brain surgery. We signed the release form with trembling hands.

Celeste was pensive as I explained to her what I thought the surgery would involve. We prayed together, our arms around each other, and then prepared to drive to the hospital for her pre-op blood tests. On the way, I asked her what she was most afraid of.

"I'm afraid of two things, Mom."

"What are they? Maybe I can help."

"Well, I don't want to give blood. All those needles hurt so bad." Tears welled up in her eyes. She had been so courageous, but even the prospect of surgery wasn't as frightening as another needle. I reassured her that the needles to take blood don't sting like those that are filled with anesthetic. That out of the way, she went on to the other thing that was troubling her.

"I want to ask you for a favor, Mom." Again, she began to cry. I reached toward her small and vulnerable form in the car seat beside me. "Mom, you gotta promise me that during the surgery tomorrow you won't cry. I just can't stand it when you cry."

My eyes filled involuntarily with tears I hoped she wouldn't notice as I realized that she was more concerned about me than herself. What a lesson in faith she was teaching me. And so, during the rest of the day, as we prepared her costume for the Halloween carnival at her school that night, as I spoke to her friends' parents about the surgery to take place the next day, I reaffirmed to her and to everyone the confidence I had that God was powerful and that He was in control.

Since I knew He was in control, I knew I could keep my promise to Celeste not to cry during her surgery. It was hard not to as she waved good-bye to us, smiling and clutching her pink teddy bear. I had brought cookies, nut bread, a large container of coffee, and juice, and as soon as Celeste disappeared behind those swinging doors, we and our friends from church had an agape feast. We kept the conversation light as we waited for news.

I had packed extra makeup in my purse. My mother had secret instructions that if the doctor had bad news, she was to keep other people away from me while I went to the hospital chapel. There I planned to scream my head off for a while and then repair my makeup. I was determined to be smiling by the time Celeste came out of the anesthesia—no matter what the prognosis.

Dan and I had bought Celeste a special Cabbage Patch baby—a little boy with a football helmet. We didn't know if she would have to wear any type of protective headgear after her surgery, and we hoped the doll would ease that eventuality. I clutched it hard against me.

I found out later that there were thousands of people praying for Celeste and Dr. Pressley during that hour. Hundreds of members of the Churches of Christ in New Mexico, Texas, Colorado, Arizona, New

York, Oklahoma, and Tennessee. A twenty-four-hour prayer chain had been holding her up since the night before, instigated by the Rev. Glen Greenwood of Ohio, with whom I was writing a book. Members of the Zondervan Publishing House staff, teachers at the Sunset School of Preaching, the gospel singing group Acappella and their staff, Catholics at special masses in Albuquerque and Santa Fe, and Christians of all different brands all over this country were praying for our little Celeste.

In fact, the atmosphere in that waiting room was one of calm and expectancy. When Dr. Pressley entered, a big smile on his face, and asked quizzically, "Is anyone in here interested in Celeste Scott?" all twenty-some-odd people in the room jumped up. He told us that the tumor had been completely removed, that it had not in any way damaged her brain, and that she had come through the surgery with the same cheerful spirit she'd had all through this trial. We were ecstatic.

I must admit I broke my promise. But it was just a tear or two—of joy, and gratitude that God had done what Celeste and I knew He could do all along.

I come now to this tenuous juncture
Where I must choose to believe.

My breast-fed faith
Is weakening

My presumed and presumptuous tenets
Are eroding like river-run flagstone,
Sloughing off like mica
And each piece is smoky-transparent

I see no end to this hurting.
I feel no confirmation of this hope
I have clutched for these long years;
Nor do require any giftings
As brideprice for the marriage
Of my faith to You.

I give You my soul:
I am not a fit caretaker anyway

Resolutely I choose to believe,
To fend off the adversary;
Even with my failing strength
I choose
To trust You.

THREE
Praise: Who Is Our God?

A friend of mine tells the story of being taken to a Texas county fair when he was a young boy. He begged and begged to ride some of the rides on the small midway, but his father, eyeing the rattle-trap contrivances, wisely refused. Then they came upon a fun house, one which was billed as a house of mirrors.

The young boy could hardly contain his excitement when his father paid his admission price and let him go into the fun house alone. His elation was mixed with a feeling of being very, very grown-up.

Just ahead was a pretty teenage girl, who, like him, was unaccompanied in the fun house. As soon as she turned the first corner, she stopped suddenly, seeing her reflection all around. She pirouetted and preened, viewing herself from all angles, adjusting her dress, smoothing her hair into place. Then, satisfied, she went on into the next room of mirrors and out of sight of the young boy.

But he hardly noticed her departure, for he too was arrested by his own multiplied image all over the room. He saw his own chubby cheeks, his wayward brown hair, his sturdy legs from angles he had never before seen. His fascination was unbounded. Time passed unnoticed in that wondrous place while he paraded and turned and gawked.

After a while he grew tired of this game and began to look for the doorway out. But there were no sills or jambs to mark the doorway. Every vertical surface was a mirror, and no matter where he turned, he saw nothing but himself. Each time he would step toward a wall, his own image would approach him, mocking him with the tears he saw beginning to run down his cheeks. His hands touched the flat, cool surfaces with smudges that, too, were reflected again and again.

He began to cry loudly, his recent feelings of maturity evaporating. Above his wails he heard a familiar sound— that of his father calling his name. He stifled his sobs and looked for the source of the sound, which seemed very close. Then he noticed something he had previously overlooked: a crack in the warped walls where they did not quite meet. He ran toward that crack still panicky, and pressed his eye to the opening.

There, outside, just inches away, was his father, speaking softly, his face also pressed to the crack. With calming words, he directed the young boy through the mirror-maze, out the final door, and into the cool night air.

That's the way crisis affects us, isn't it? Sometimes we find ourselves in the middle of a difficult situation because we insisted on putting ourselves there. Sometimes we are propelled there unknowingly or unwillingly and find that our surroundings are a new world that bears little resemblance to what we're used to.

Some people, like the teenage girl in the fun house, are able to keep their bearings and use the time to look objectively at themselves. They make changes and corrections according to what they see, and then they somehow find their way out. These are usually people who have been in such a place before.

But most of us are like my young friend. Such disorientating experiences make us focus on ourselves. We look at ourselves, sometimes as if from a distance, as we go through the automatic motions that get us through one day at a time, one action at a time. At first, we are fascinated by what we see ourselves doing. We congratulate ourselves on our equilibrium or mourn the effects of shock or loss on our minds.

We ask questions like, *Why is this happening to me? Why not to someone else? How will this affect my future?* Sometimes even the experience of suffering becomes itself a drug with which we sedate ourselves, observing how we react.

But there comes a time when we tire of this narcissistic gazing on our own image. Then, when the reality of our situation becomes an inevitability, we start searching for ways out of the hurting, in previously unnoticed corners where the mirrors don't block the view.

For a Christian, there is always a soft voice calling his or her name. There is someone outside this maze of our lives who not only knows the way out, but wants to guide us there and stands ready to welcome us with open arms.

But what if He were a practical joker? Could we trust His directions? Would His calling our name be a comfort or a derision?

This must be considered when we are in the bedlam of crisis, for how a Christian handles such times is often determined by how he or she envisions the God outside our mirrored walls.

The privilege we Christians have of approaching this all-seeing Being in a way that allows us to call Him our Father is a new thing, relatively speaking; Old Testament believers didn't address Him that way. To them, He was indeed powerful and undefeatable, even loving, but the intimacy of seeing Him as a parent was unthinkable. That is why the Jews of Jesus' day were shocked when He called God His father and doubly shocked when He taught His disciples to pray to "our Father."

Of course, much has been written about how we humans relate to this Father-God based on how we relate to our earthly fathers. Once this Father-father tie is acknowledged, though, we make compensations for our imperfect earthly parents and carry on from there.

J. B. Phillips, in his book *Your God Is Too Small*, has outlined various different mental images we have of God. Among them are the Resident Policeman, the Parental Hangover, the Grand Old Man, Meek and Mild, Absolute Perfection, the Heavenly Bosom, God-in-a-Box, Managing

Director, Second-Hand God, Perennial Grievance, Pale Galilean, the Projected Image, and other idols that reflect our own value systems.

The image that each of us has of God seems to evolve with each passing day, adjusting to whatever experiences we have. It seems to me, however, that a crisis situation "freezes" this evolution, like a stop-action camera. Feelings and fears we may have hidden or ignored regarding God float to the surface. It may be the first time in our lives that we have to deal directly with this God that we have built.

In a bad situation, one that is beyond our control, we naturally want God to step in and fix up the mess. After all, Christians who have paid their dues and punched the timeclock of church attendance feel entitled to some special considerations. But we usually find to our dismay that such considerations are hard to find, if indeed they exist.

Well-meaning friends say to just grit our teeth and praise God—He's doing the best thing in our lives. Whether we are able to praise God in the middle of a maelstrom involves an assessment of what kind of a God He is: before you praise, you must first appraise.

Breaking my assumptions about Him down into steps has been helpful to me. By going through these steps, I can find out at which point I am having problems with thinking correctly about Him and His role in my life.

The first step is acknowledging that God even knows about my situation. Well, I assume, He knows everything. So on to step two: Does He care?

If He cared enough to let His Son die, then surely He cares about my problem. But if He cares, why doesn't He do something about it? Step three: *Can* He do something about it? (When I concluded that God, in giving Celeste a successful recovery from her surgery, was doing what I knew He could do, I was acknowledging His ability; His ultimate intention was another matter entirely.)

Evaluating that God knows, cares, and is able to do something for my crisis is very unsatisfying when hours and weeks and months and sometimes even years drag by with no visible intervention. We approach step four—the evaluation of His motives—hesitantly but sometimes inevitably, finding ourselves wondering like the Old Testament writers if God has become distracted or has fallen asleep. Is He a well-meaning, informed bumbler who misfiled our case and won't return our calls?

Our reason rejects such thinking and yet our hearts waver. Most of us find ourselves right in the middle of step five—waiting. Deciding that God is aware and caring and able and responsible is fairly easy, once we think about it. But we are nose-to-nose with the reality that our situation seems to be unchanged. We feel we have been placed against our will in suspended animation, pending uncontrollable action at some unforeseeable date.

Here is where the Christian makes the mental decision—the crux— that will make the difference. The first option is to decide that this situation will eventually be resolved and to adopt a "fortress mentality" to survive until that resolution. In looking back over my own life, I recognize this state of mind—I lived there for a week while five-month-old Celeste fought for her life under an oxygen tent with pneumonia. I felt a victim of a situation from which God had inexplicably withdrawn. I didn't resent it nor fight against it. I felt instead stunned and dazed, prepared for any outcome, cut off from a distant God who had no reason I could think of for getting involved. This situation has become in my own personal history the definition of blind faith, and I see my brothers and sisters living in this netherland day after day.

But there is a better way—the way of informed faith. Informed faith is based on knowing God and the absolute assurance that He is not waiting to take action in our lives; He is at any given moment already doing something.

The question then becomes not a matter of whether or not He knows about our situation; the reality is that He knew before we were born that this would arise and throughout our lives He has been making provisions, unbeknownst to us, for its victorious resolution. Wondering if He cares is replaced by an assurance that He is already working. "Can He help me" is swallowed up by an expectant eye toward how much He is helping.

When we moved back to Albuquerque in June of 1986, I shared this kind of thinking with my children while we packed. As they mused about what kind of a house we would buy, I told them that not only did God have a place prepared for us, He even knew the exact address and phone number we would have. Perhaps the owner of our "new" house might not even know that he would be moving out, I assured them, but God did.

It was one thing to blithely say this, but as the months dragged on and our house in Boulder did not sell, the process of praising God (saying that He is powerful and wants good things for us, knowing He had always taken care of our needs, concluding that He would once again do so) became a little more difficult. We were here in Albuquerque living with my mother and brother—four adults and two large children and lots of furniture in a house designed for one family. It crossed my mind that whatever house God had prepared for us must be pretty special because it was taking an awfully long time to present itself. We couldn't buy it until we sold our Boulder home, and week after week went by without a buyer. With varying degrees of success I stifled the urge to feel sorry for myself.

Then, suddenly, the months of preparation that God had been making went from the invisible realm to the visible. A house I had long admired just down the street from our church and school went on the market. The day we viewed it and discovered how perfectly arranged— and priced—it was, we returned to my mother's home and found that our Boulder realtor had called during our absence, saying she had a firm offer on the house there.

Both deals went off without a hitch until the man who was selling his home to us developed a stubborn streak and refused to move out until a month after we had to vacate our Boulder home. We were in limbo once more. Again, I wondered what God was up to.

Midnight a few nights later provided the answer. I heard my mother screaming and crying in the bedroom next to us. A persistent backache had worsened, and she had herniated a disk in her back. She spent a week in the hospital, and when she returned home, I was able (and happy) to provide the services of cooking, cleaning, marketing, and driving her to daily therapy sessions. It was easy—she was right there in the same house. Had we moved into our new home, I would have surely worn myself out driving back and forth, cooking duplicate meals, cleaning two houses. God had known that all along.

He was gracious enough, in addition, to permit me to see His hand in these situations. I knew that honoring Him by verbalizing my faith in Him ahead of time—consciously praising Him—did not bind Him to a set agenda I had in mind. He knew much better than I what was best. This revelation of His hand was no freebie, however; I know I must use it as I reassess Him in the future.

C. S. Lewis acknowledged this painful dynamic in a relationship with God when he noted in *A Grief Observed*, "My idea of God is not a divine idea. It has to be shattered time after time. He shatters it Himself. He is the great iconoclast."

In the same book, Lewis pointed out that even people whom we know well will often do or say things that we regard as out of character for them. How much more so the incomprehensible God. We can assess "how He is" because of past exhibitions of His behavior in our lives, but we must always leave room for His divine prerogative of doing things we do not understand because He is Himself beyond our understanding.

Our knowledge-based generation is frustrated by a quantity that on this earth will always be at least partially unknown.

We often find to our dismay that in crisis, God is a God of surprises. Many times, they are not the serendipitous outcome of events—they are jarring surprises like ruined health and shattered dreams and even death. Many a sufferer in hospitals and nursing homes across this country would tell you bitterly that they never expected things to turn out the way they did.

I do not pretend to have answers for why God does what He does or allows what He allows. I admit that many things I know He can prevent still happen. I am continually surprised, so to speak, by the events that take place in this world. But the surprises are in what I see, not in what He is.

Many people in the Bible acknowledged that they were at a loss to explain why God sometimes acts the way He does. Already alluded to was Psalm 44:23-24, where the psalmist wondered if perhaps the Lord were asleep, chiding, "Awake, O Lord! Why do you sleep? Rouse yourself!"

Even longsuffering Jeremiah once compared God to an overnight visitor, a stranger in the land who would move on as soon as morning came (Jeremiah 14:8), and anyone who has tried to maintain equilibrium in a continuing bad situation would identify with his feelings.

Isaiah told of how some of his people would go out into a forest where they cut down trees they found there. Then they would take part of the wood and build a fire to warm up from their activities. Then they would bake themselves some bread and, with fire-warmed fingers and baked-bread fullness, would proceed to carve the remainder of the wood into something to bow down to and say to, "Save me; you are my god."

We twentieth-century Christians laugh smugly at such silliness as all the while we order our lives by a parceled-out God we create in our own minds. We see Him as utilitarian as that block of wood. We'll feast on

His promises to take care of His children; warm (and sometimes even cauterize) our consciences with the knowledge that His judgment will "take care of" evil people we don't choose to deal with; and then throw ourselves down before the chipped-away image of a God who will always give us a second chance and special privileges. When lean times come or evil people prosper or we must suffer the consequences of our own foolish actions, we are powerless to reconcile these realities in our lives with the multiplied mental snapshots we have in our minds of the different gods we serve.

But lest we be too hard on ourselves, we can take some comfort from the fact that even those people who companied with the God-on-earth in three years of daily life also did not have accurate views of who he was. John, for instance, knew Jesus intimately. He had fished with Him, eaten with Him, slept beside Him. He had seen His gentle and angry attitudes. He had seen Him resplendent in His Shechinah glory on the Mount of Transfiguration and later, beaten and bloodied in the courtyard of the high priest.

He saw Him live and then he saw Him die. He saw the tomb filled with its precious contents, and its gaping emptiness on the third morning. Then John saw Him resurrected, touched Him, ate the fish He roasted on the sandy beach, and finally watched His pierced feet disappear into the clouds over his head.

Yes, John knew Jesus was God; but more important, he knew Jesus. But everything he thought he knew about the Jesus to whom he had devoted his whole life—all the sum of his memories and experiences—was eclipsed by contact with Him. When John saw the magnificent, glorified Being that addressed him on the isle of Patmos, John fell over in a swoon, as if dead.

Not exactly a breathy "Praise the Lord," was it? His reaction mirrored that of Isaiah, who in the same situation cried out, "I am ruined!" and Ezekiel, who like John fell flat on his face in terror.

The action of these men—good, godly men favored by God—make us realize that knowing God will not have the immediate effect of making us comfortable in His presence. Part of that is because, as already noted, we can never hope to completely comprehend Him. But more important is the fact that we can never approach Him as our equal.

Consciously we know that fact. But in the middle of crisis, we tend to slide into the thinking that we have a reciprocal agreement with God; that we shook hands at our conversion and because we kept our end of the deal by "being good," He was bound to do for us what we think is best. When this fails to happen, it is rarely our conception of the deal that we blame—it is our Partner. We conveniently forget that He put up His Son's blood as surety on this negotiation and has guaranteed it with His Spirit as an earnest. Were it not for His continuously erased account books, we'd be in debt to Him from now till forever.

Praising God—saying what is true of Him—involves knowing Him first. We dare not try to verbalize or even conceptualize praise to God if we do it thinking that knowing Him accurately is only optional.

I say "we dare not" advisedly—not because I believe that God will send a bolt of lightning to stop us in midsentence if we come to Him in deliberate ignorance. We dare not because of the devastatingly stunting effect this will have on our relationship for the rest of our lives if it is continued.

I can say with certainty that my own relationship with God, rich and full though I feel it is, has lagged far behind what it could have been and should have been at this point in my life, because of years of misconceptions about who God is.

Those who have read my first book, *The Mormon Mirage*, know that I spent ten years of my life as a faithful Mormon. The God of Mormonism is vastly different from the God worshiped by mainstream Christians. Mormons reject the idea of a trinitarian Deity, asserting that God the

Father, Jesus, and the Holy Spirit are each separate beings, each with a distinct body.

They teach that the personage they address as God the Father was once a man who lived on a faraway earth, died, was resurrected, and was given godhood by his own earth's god as a reward for his obedient life. The personage they refer to as Jesus was created by God the Father. The Holy Spirit of Mormonism, bound by the spiritual body he possesses, cannot indwell anyone and is only perceived by his influence on people.

It was very easy for me to visualize and believe in these three very finite beings. I prayed only to the Father, accepting the teaching that Jesus was subordinate to the Father.

Then when I became a Christian, I found that the Bible taught clearly that there are not and never were any other gods than the triune God of the Bible. The Son Jesus is the Father God's equal and was no more created at any point in time than the Father was; and the Holy Spirit can indeed indwell and help me individually.

It is one thing to mentally accept these facts when presented with the plain teaching of the Bible on these inarguable points. It is quite another to go from worshiping three concrete, tangible people to directing my attention to a multifaceted invisible eternal God. It would be as if someone came up to you and was able to convince you beyond a doubt that every photograph and painting of the Taj Mahal was inaccurate. Somehow someone was able through all these years to perpetrate a fraud on the American people by trickery and fake camera angles to convince them that it existed when it did not. Then imagine being asked to believe in a far more lovely building, hidden high in an inaccessible mountain cliff, whose reflection could be seen, which cast breathlessly beautiful shadows, but which no one had ever actually seen. "Just imagine pure beauty," someone might say. "Or truth embodied," another might tell you. "But forget the years you spent admiring the Taj

Mahal, because it doesn't exist," you'd be warned, "you're just wasting your time."

There are, I freely admit, problems with such an analogy, but it does reflect the dilemma of those who have to change their entire conception of God in spiritual midstream. When we do not see God as he really is, the pain of such a change is surpassed only by its necessity.

Nor can such a change be effected overnight. We do not—indeed we cannot—throw out entire thought patterns when we discover that they are based on falsehood. Whether the lie is that God is a former man or an impersonal force or a jeweled statue, such a lie will affect the way we think about everything in our lives, to one degree or another.

Like a cancer—indeed, more than a cancer—such things must be cut out of our lives and our thinking. God absolutely demands, according to Jesus, to be worshiped in spirit and in truth.

Where do you start to find this truth? If you want to learn the true nature of a person you know only slightly, do you not listen to what he says? Watch him carefully as he interacts with others? Find out how he reacts when he is pleased, sad, angry? The record of God's behavior, the Bible, tells us these things about the way He reacts to people and to ideas. There is no excuse for a twentieth-century believer talking about not knowing and loving God if he or she willfully neglects the Word, which is the mind of God in written form. In reading the Bible, a picture emerges of a complex and wondrous Personality, strong and loving. As we read, we make mental lists of those things that are undeniably true about Him.

Seeing Him accurately and acknowledging what we see is the basis of all praise.

Praise is the foundation of all relationship and communication with God.

And communication and relationship with God are the only hope, the only sure anchor a Christian can depend on when faced with crisis.

He is the Mighty One
He is the Creator
The Great One

He who can bring victory
Out of the mingled paste
Of blood and ashes of defeat

How do I know
How can I say this

I stand with my elbows touching
Those of sorrowing men and women
Frozen in a slice of Friday-time
When all the world's hopes
Were laid in a hastily-washed heap
In a borrowed tomb

With no hope
No hope

No hope

Until the first rays of Sunday
Bathed the empty tomb ledge

FOUR

Praise: What He's Done in the Past

There is a worn green file folder at the back of the top drawer of my gray metal filing cabinet—the cabinet where I file papers relating to my writing. This file folder holds papers and cards of all sizes, shapes, and colors. They are not arranged chronologically or according to the senders. In fact, they are not arranged at all.

I can't remember the last time I took this file folder out and actually looked at its contents, but I add papers to it on a fairly regular basis—whenever they arrive in the mail or are pressed into my hand after I have spoken publicly somewhere. This file folder holds letters and notes from people who have read what I have written and have responded to it.

One letter in particular is vivid in my memory. It is from a man in South Africa. When I think of this letter, I am overwhelmed with praise for a God who is so caring, so provident, that He would send some of my attempts to understand Him and His world halfway around that world to a man who had been praying for someone to help him understand too.

I know that my writing is not what is significant about this folder. What is important is the way that God guided my writing into the hands of people who needed it, just at the right time in their lives.

I said that I rarely ever actually look into that folder—perhaps the last time I did so was over a year ago when I rearranged my filing system. But that folder is often on my mind. Each time I sit before the unblinking green eye of my computer monitor and wonder to myself, "What's the use? Does anyone really care what I write?" I remember the smooth bulk of that folder, and I am encouraged once again to write.

Most of us have a mental filing system, much like my cabinet, whether we realize it or not. In separate "folders" in our minds, we categorize our life experiences and put them together with things of a similar nature. Sometimes our filing system may not make much sense when we think about it, for we may have lumped our own bad experiences together with the social injustices of the world, even though they may not really have much in common. But in our private systems, logic usually doesn't count for much.

Much of our self-image as well as our view of the world around us and the God who rules it is determined not so much by what is in those mental files, but by how we handle them. I maintain some emotional equilibrium, for instance, by not looking at the also-bulging file I have of rejection slips from editors and publishers. Others, too, may acknowledge the presence in their lives of past bad experiences, but choose to focus on the present and the future.

Both kinds of files are necessary to a Christian, though, because they reflect both the actions of God in our lives and our reactions to Him.

You will recall that in the previous chapter we concentrated on the first element of praise: acknowledging who God is. In our mental filing folder under "God" we file the information that we know about His nature (who He is) and His character (how He expresses His nature through actions and teachings about Himself). Knowing God accurately is vital: this file must contain only truth, or we will misfile or even throw away all the other information we receive about Him.

Sometimes when we are confronted with an overwhelming situation unlike an we've ever faced before, we make the mistake of unconsciously thinking that the God to whom we must appeal today is somehow different from the God of yesterday. We "forget" that God is not created anew for each new trial. He is literally the same yesterday, today, and tomorrow. The young boy David, eyeing the monstrous giant Goliath, knew this truth—He said that the same God who had rescued him from the paw of the lion and the paw of the bear in very real past experiences would show Himself consistent by rescuing him from that new brute (1 Samuel 17:37).

With this statement David also illuminated another truth, this time not just about God, but about us too; he showed that we are inclined to judge the future actions of someone by their past actions. Even God does that when dealing with us humans, David noted in Psalm 18:25-26:

> To the faithful you show yourself faithful,
>> to the blameless you show yourself blameless,
> to the pure you show yourself pure,
>> but to the crooked you show yourself shrewd.

In human-to-human relationships, we find that we are often mistaken about the actions of other people or our interpretations of them. Then, too, people change. But God does not.

In fact, God wants us to look to His past actions and draw conclusions about Him from them. He recognized long ago that we become discouraged and need to have reassurance. For instance, when John, Jesus' beloved cousin, was in prison, he apparently started having second thoughts about Jesus being the Messiah. When John sent his disciples to Jesus to ask if He was the one to come or if they should expect someone else, Jesus didn't respond with a list of prophecies from the Old Testament or a litany of His divine attributes of love and grace. "Go back and report to John," Jesus replied, "what you hear and see: The blind receive sight, the lame walk, those who have leprosy are cured, the deaf hear, the dead are raised, and the good news is preached to the poor" (Matthew 11:4-5). Jesus wanted John to draw his own conclusions about Jesus' divinity on the basis of what He did, not just what He said— and what is even more marvelous, He wanted that information filtered through the mesh of human experience. The medium He chose was communication, human to human, about what they had seen and heard.

That wasn't the only time Jesus appealed to human memory to establish the reality of His power in their minds. You will recall that later, when the disciples were hungry, He turned their memories back to the time when He had miraculously fed thousands. "Don't you remember," He chided, "the five loaves for the five thousand, and how many basketfuls you gathered? Or the seven loaves for the four thousand, and how many basketfuls you gathered?" (Matthew 16:9-10).

I am deeply moved by the fact that all we know of God from beyond our own lifespans has come through human memory. You know, God could have zapped the Holy Bible into existence like He did other things at creation. Instead, He chose to talk to people, to give them life-changing experiences, and then to let them convey these things to the rest of us. Some of those people, like Matthew and Mark, were eyewitnesses to what they wrote. Others, like the writers of Genesis and Luke, were just the recipients of the memory banks of others. The end result is the same: The Holy Spirit worked within those individual memories and personalities to transmit what God wanted us to know.

Just because it has come to us in a lump is no good reason to treat it as a lump, but we do. We see the experiences of those people as far removed from our own; their God a God of the past. (But the Spirit nags our minds with "Yesterday, today, tomorrow . . .")

The truth is that God is daily writing our own history in our hearts and memories. The introduction to this our inner book, the basis for all the coming information and conclusions, is His character as He has shown Himself to countless other humans, just like us, throughout time. What we learn about Him in Scripture is unimpeachably reliable, the foundation for the interpretation of all following deductions we draw about our own lives. If indeed He does not change and if indeed He has been merciful to those who depended on Him in the past to help with their crises, then, I must assume, He will do the same for you and me.

That the nature of God is inextricably tied up with the nature of praise is undeniable. Deuteronomy 10:21 tells us that God is praise and then follows this definition of Deity with the seal of human experience— "He is your God, who performed for you those great and awesome wonders you saw with your own eyes."

The Old Testament Jews knew well this concept of a personal history. They defined not only their God, but themselves as well by looking at the way God had interacted with them. Again and again throughout the Old Testament they referred to that marvelous experience of crossing the Red Sea and used it as a rallying point of experience to encourage each other with the fact that if He could do such wonders in the past, surely He could do them in their present. But they also recognized that this history was not a static thing; that new chapters were to be written on the compelling theme of God's love. The Jews of Jeremiah's day, for instance, were told that the day of their deliverance would be a day in which both their self-image and their reputation as a nation would forever change. From that point on they would no longer be known just as the people of the escape from Egypt, but the people recovered from the northlands exile too (Jeremiah 23:7-8).

Like David, we must keep a count of the lions' and bears' paws from which we have been delivered in our lives; like the Jews we must acknowledge the Egyptians and Babylonians of our own histories who would surely have destroyed us were it not for God's grace. In practical terms, it is one thing to memorize a list of God's divine attributes; it is quite another to be able to point to the acting-out of His character at specific times in our own lives.

How can we do this? Or returning to the analogy of the file folders, how do we reach into these dusty places and make the experiences of the past useful to us right now? One way is to depend on human memory—by asking someone who is spiritually mature to recount for you the times that God has rescued him or her. Many Christians who are older than you in the faith will be happy to share rich memories of the otherwise inexplicable times in their lives that God intervened to their benefit. I myself have multiple volumes of "blank books" that I have used for years now to record prayer requests I have made of God. I am greatly encouraged by (and love to encourage others with) this physical evidence I can hold in my hands, marked with dates, times, and situations, showing how God has indeed responded to crises in my life and in the lives of others I know.

Other Christians too will point out at your request particular Scriptures that were "just what they needed" in a do-or-die situation. In fact, many people do what I do when a Scripture seems unusually appropriate for me—mark down the date and place when you read it. A Bible so marked becomes a knitted-together garment of the threads of your life and those of Scripture, sweet with the fragrance of praise, a tangible and warming symbol of the workings of the God of the Bible in your own history.

This process of asking for and accepting the testimony of the past alerts us that we have passed through a threshold in the defining of praise: once you have accurately apprehended the nature of God and have mentally acknowledged that this nature has demonstrated itself in history, then the next logical step is vocalizing these things. Here is where most people understand the concept of praise—in what Myrna Alexander in *Behold Your God* identifies as the basic meaning of the word praise, being "confession in the sense of declaration."

In literature we speak of a literary device known as a *synecdoche*, in which a part of something becomes a symbol for the whole. We use the phrase "all hands on deck" when we are referring to the sailors whose hands will do the swabbing; we understand a complete fallen nature—

not only of the vision—when John speaks of the "lust of the eyes." In many ways, the concept that first pops into the minds of Christians when they hear the word "praise"—a concept that includes the visual image of someone saying complimentary things about or to God, perhaps even raising up hands in a group setting—has become a Christian's *synecdoche* for the entire, multilayered biblical definition of praise. In fact, as we have seen, vocalizing praise is only a third step that must be preceded by knowing God and acknowledging His power in the past—and is not even the end of the process, at that.

Yet since it is the most familiar and visible manifestation of praise to most people, it deserves our attention. Saying what is true, what is in the heart, as Jesus tersely noted in Matthew 12:34, is automatic, whether what overflows is good or bad. Unshared praise is by definition fallacious.

Yet where did we ever get the idea that we are doing God a favor by admitting what is true of Him? In so doing we only cut our losses like the manager in Luke 16; like the unprofitable servants of Luke 17:10, we have only done our duty. Nonetheless, in crisis, this duty is sometimes almost unbearably heavy. When we are faced with unmoving realities such as death or suffering, the potential comfort we might draw from the concept of an all-powerful God who is not removed from our situation is a comfort we are wont to refuse. The giddy hours of blithely saying how good He is seem distant and irrelevant.

It is at such a crossroads—one at which I have often stood—that other realities must supersede, and at which the advantage of dealing with a known quantity of dependable goodness takes precedence over our own feelings. Just as marriages are not held together by the memory of the hormonal rush of the first kiss, so too the glue of our relationship with God in the rocky times must be knowledge of His nature, not just our feelings about Him. Sometimes—and I am ashamed to admit it— my praise to God has begun through clenched teeth; for this unprofitable servant, even my duty was, at least at first, an overwhelming task.

Does God accept such reluctant praising? Surely He is not impressed with empty words. But for me the process of praise in a crisis situation sometimes begins as an act not only of self-discipline, but also as the first step in allowing Him to comfort me. Without any doubt the benefits to me of reminding myself of what kind of a God He is, and of how He has shown that nature to others and to me, are much greater than the potentially good effect of such grudging statements on Him.

In such cases, I offer the pet lamb of my own pride and anger to Him who certainly does not need this or anything else upon the altar of my relationship to Him. Thus, it is in crisis that we learn in the heart, not in the mind, what the writer in Hebrews 13:15 meant by the phrase, "a sacrifice of praise."

Our praise must always rise above our feelings and inclinations, if for no other reason than our own good; if we praise only when we are feeling high, then we judge ourselves for being low and the consequent damage that can be done by our lack of communication with our God.

Indeed, we find ourselves sometimes helplessly bound by our misconceptions about praise. By mistakenly linking it . with emotions, we associate it with thankfulness, with wonder, with enthusiasm, and with a loving submission to God. All these emotions can quite properly be involved in biblical praise, but not necessarily so. Many people have a vague feeling of thankfulness for a sunny day for their picnic without ever consciously acknowledging the God of the sun. The Israelites of Psalm 105:23-45 were repeatedly awestruck by God's power, but their flattery didn't qualify as praise, at least in His eyes. David's resignation and submission to God after the death of his infant son showed recognition of God's power and his relationship to God, but it could hardly be seen as enthusiastic.

And finally, one of the most stirring praise passages of the Old Testament, tinged with the bittersweet flavor of firsthand experience, was uttered by an uncircumcised Babylonian ruler who, as far as we know, never completely submitted to God except when forced to:

> His dominion is an eternal dominion;
>   His kingdom endures from generation to generation.
> All the peoples of the earth are regarded as nothing.
> He does as He pleases . with the powers of heaven
>   and the peoples of the earth.
> No one can hold back his hand or say to him,
>   "What have you done?"
> . . . Now I, Nebuchadnezzar, praise and exalt and glorify
> the King of heaven, because everything he does is right
> and all his ways are just. And those who walk in pride he
> is able to humble.
>
> Daniel 4:34-35, 37

Well, perhaps our grudging praise—and subsequent wholehearted submission—are not so distasteful to Him after all.

2 CORINTHIANS 1:20

This is no vengeful deity
Who cuts off the outstretched hand

This is not a capricious idol
Who plays chess with men's souls;
No eternal checkmate

This is no prankster God
Who twists words
And impales them upon intents

This is He
Who knows needs before they're perceived
Who grants favors as they're verbalized
Who invites us to believe
In what cannot be
Just so that He can make it
So:

This is the mighty God
Of the perpetual
Yes

FIVE

Praise: What He Will Do in the Future

Viktor Frankl was imprisoned by the Nazis during World War II. In spite of the incredible hardships he endured, he remained alert and observed the actions and reactions of many of his fellow captives.

Sustained imprisonment affects people differently. As these prisoners were stripped of their roles in society, of their possessions, of their health, of necessities such as food and clothing, and in most cases, ultimately of their lives, many were completely broken. Others, though, seemed to rise above it in a way that Frankl found remarkable. He noticed that some of the men in the camp would, on a regular basis, choose to give their only food to a weaker prisoner. The nourishment they lost was somehow offset in their minds by the exercising of this ability. The last freedom, Frankl concluded as he observed this, is *the freedom to choose one's attitudes.*

A Christian who is familiar with the Bible knows that as far as praise goes, Jesus will eventually get it from every human being. Sometimes it is easy to misinterpret the weight of this—and see Jesus in the role of the glowering TV mechanic who mutters, "Pay me now or pay me later." (And we know that "later" is always going to be worse.) The same God who saw His people ignoring His commands to let the land rest every seven years and who recouped 490 years of such rebellion by sending His people away for 70 years—this same God assures us that every knee will bow and every tongue will confess that Jesus is Lord. But such praise, if first offered at that time, will not be offered just through clenched teeth, but through teeth that will grind throughout eternity.

Those who are undergoing crisis realize that bad circumstances tend to highlight our Christian character. Frankl's fellow prisoners' giving away of bread would be unremarkable in a place where all were well-fed and comfortable; praise when life is going well is just a foregone conclusion.

It is in the crucible of crisis that all the dross of frivolity about our relationship with God is seared out of us. In it we learn not just about our goals, purposes, attitudes, interests, feelings, and beliefs, but our values—which are different from these other things—are laid bare by the hot blast of crisis. Counselors use a description of the formation of values, called Rath's Seven-Step Process, to show how such values are created. A value must (1) be freely chosen; (2) be chosen from among other alternatives; (3) be chosen not impulsively but after reflection on possible consequences; (4) become prized and cherished; (5) be publicly affirmed to others; (6) be incorporated into actual behavior; and finally, (7) be reaffirmed and repeated in one's life.

Praise in our lives becomes a value when it goes through that process. Even though, as Henry Kissinger noted, "the absence of alternatives clears the mind marvelously," a lack of choice in praising doesn't do much for solidifying it as a helpful part of our lives. It must be consciously, lovingly chosen as a lifestyle, repeated and affirmed, in order to be valid.

But as we have seen before, sometimes crisis doesn't wait in suspended animation while we "catch up" on establishing praise as a lifestyle. The screech of brakes, a doctor's visit, or a heartbreaking phone call can change a life. Even if we recognize the need for praise (in all its fullest meaning) just as a spiritual survival technique, sometimes several of the seven steps get scrunched together in a seizure of emotion while we try to handle our unhandleable situations.

The "I adore" of other times becomes an urgent "I need." The "You are" of yesterday is replaced with "You have to." The litany becomes me, me, me. Surely, we would reason—if reasoning at such a time were possible—surely God can get along without compliments from me for a while.

Our need becomes a towering monolith on the horizon of our sight. Unless all the other background has been painted by God, His appearance on such a landscape is either an intrusion on our suffering, a terrible tease, or else an untried life preserver thrown to us on the choppy waves.

A nonbeliever in crisis may approach for the first time the presence of God in his or her life. I know several people of my own generation who see no need for God because they have been able to supply their own needs themselves; they are healthy, well-fed, have never experienced war, are satisfied in their jobs. I fear for such people, for their first experience with crisis, which will surely come, will be all the harder because it will be something for which they have had little preparation. In it, though, they may feel a need for God.

For the Christian, however, it is assumed that we have "met God" at some prior time and this should make a difference in how we would handle crisis. If that relationship with God has been cool and distant, then crisis can be a time to be reconciled to Him.

In speaking of non-Christians who have felt no need for God and of Christians who have distanced themselves from God, I am trying to put the best possible face on the ultimate results of dealing with crisis by seeking God in the midst of it. We would all agree that the right relationship with God is justified by anything we might have to overcome to achieve it. But it would be unrealistic to picture as desirable the process of dealing with a two-front war wherein we are battling the outward circumstances as well as waging war on our own spiritual battlegrounds. I can't imagine anything more hellish than such a situation—trying to decide whether to fight or be reconciled to circumstances beyond my control and trying to decide to fight or be reconciled to a God who is also beyond my control.

I have read of research done by people who clinically observe others going through trauma and grief, documenting various stages that they have observed. When confronted with a loss, people react with disbelief (even denial), try to affix blame, withdraw from others. I have felt these feelings myself at such times. There is another common reaction, however, which relates directly to the concept of biblical praise, that deserves a closer look: a response known as bargaining.

If praise indeed means we should vocalize our understanding of the nature of God, acknowledge what He has done in the past, and draw a conclusion about what He will do for me—then right now, in my crisis, what does that mean? Does it mean I should go to Scripture, find a story about someone in a situation similar to mine, and expect that the same God who acted then will do the exact same thing for me today? Would I have been justified, for instance, after looking at the story of Jesus healing the official's son in John 4, in concluding that if I approached Jesus in prayer, He would be bound to do the same for my Celeste?

Our common sense and our experience tell us that this could not be so. But when we are desperate, any weapon will do, and we can be tempted to bludgeon even God with His own past, with His own promises.

But what about those promises, the ones that assure a believer of health, prosperity, and aid? Are they only for the good times when their price is cheap and not for the bad times when we would mortgage anything to pay their inaccessible fee?

This is when the bargaining takes over. We assume the covenant we made with God at our conversion entitles us to certain rights. After all, we are children of the King and the Bride of Christ and joint heirs of the Kingdom and dearly beloved and bought with a price—doesn't that count for anything when we need to turn in our chips?

Ah, but we have misunderstood the meaning of the word covenant. According to William Barclay, the Greek word for the kind of covenant we usually have in mind is *suntheke*—an agreement between two equals, such as a marriage covenant or a treaty between two countries. But this word is not the one used in the New Testament to describe our covenant with God—that word is *diatheke*. A *diatheke* is the type of covenant that we refer to as a will. It has two outstanding characteristics. First, it is never an agreement between equals, nor can it ever be repaid. (Who of us inherits money and tries to pay it back to the rich uncle who left it to us?) Second of all, and almost too obvious to mention, is the fact that any benefits awarded in such a covenant are unilaterally decided upon, and somebody has to die to put it into effect.

Our covenant with God went into effect when Somebody died two thousand years ago on a cross. We, of course, were unaware of the legacy left to us until we accepted it the day we became His legal heirs.

All right, we concede. So He doesn't owe us anything. But why, if we believe He is unchanging and consistent, why won't He do for me in my hour of need what He did for others in the past?

To answer this, we must again return to the basis of praise: who God is. We want so badly to skip this part and go right on to what He has done in the past. We want to take the threads of His relationship with us and tie Him down like Gulliver until He agrees to do things our way.

Psalm 115:3 assures us that "He does whatever pleases Him." If I, like the ancient Greeks and Romans, see God as a glorified human in my own image, then I am right in being terrified by the prospect of a capricious and arbitrary deity, for who could predict what would please him?

Where is the anchor in such a sea of confusion? I found such an anchor in Psalm 62:11-12. "You, O God, are strong" (else why would I have confidence in asking You for help?)—but more important, "You, O Lord, are loving."

Loving. That means He knows me intimately. Loving. That means He cares about what is happening to me. Loving. And love is always followed by action, which means He is actively doing something—right now—to help me handle this mess.

The "mighty hand and outstretched arm" of God are mentioned over and over in the Psalms. God Himself repeatedly drew attention to this visual image of His great strength. But how must it make Him feel when we reduce Him to a dismembered appendage on which we call when we need help?

Few of us would choose to be immortalized for a single act we have done in our lives, no matter how noble that act; for surely honesty and modesty would compel us to be known rather as complete people. Without discounting the great importance of each individual act God performed in history, we must nonetheless turn away from these single recountings to see Him, too, as He chose to be seen—in repeated acts of service throughout history that draw attention ultimately away from His hand to His heart, His love for us.

In practical terms, that means I must indeed stake my spiritual future on His past—but not on His past actions, but rather on His past (and therefore present and future) nature. In crisis I return to the stairsteps of my own faith wherein I reaffirm to myself and to anyone else who needs it my well-worn catechism: that there is a God, He is a good God, He knows about my problem, He can be depended upon, and finally the faith-stretching admission that He is at every juncture of crisis actively doing something that will help me. Not, I agree, an easy bill to fill, but the only option for sanity and equilibrium for a Christian.

This does not mean that Christians in crisis should throw up their hands and wait for God to take care of everything. By some people's definition it might have been "an act of faith" for me to have done such a thing when I discovered the tumor on Celeste's skull, but I believe my "faith" would have cost her dearly. Of course God could have compensated for my actions. But I myself would have felt irresponsible, and I don't enjoy the thought of making God "clean up after me." Like Moses, we who are faced with great trial can first of all answer God's question: "What is that in your hand?" and use what we already possess to show ourselves God's co-workers in our situations.

But I believe that inherent in the very definition of crisis is the idea that it is something we cannot fix or handle alone. When our ammunition is gone, our armories depleted, then the realization of helplessness slaps us in the face; and often we find that we are unable to lift even our hands against this most invincible of enemies.

There are two ways to deal with an enemy like helplessness, against whom there can be no victory. One is to rage against it (and often this alone has its own satisfaction, at least for a while). But Abraham Lincoln spoke of another strategy that in the long run is more productive: that of destroying an enemy by making it a friend.

But, we protest, a friend should be an aid to us, a comfort, a companion. How can helplessness become a friend?

Perhaps the greatest service that such a feeling can do for us is turn us toward God. Since crises are by definition those situations that are unhandleable, then recognizing our own limitations is bound to save us frustration and wasted energy. Not only that, but Christians all over the world share the conclusion I have come to after each crisis: once I recognized that God—not I—was in control, I felt relieved and confident in Him.

But another thought is bound to occur to any Christian. If one of the desired end results of crisis in a Christian's life is a renewal of praise, couldn't He figure out a way to get us to praise Him that didn't hurt so badly?

Warren and Ruth Myers in their book *Praise: A Door to God's Presence* explain the great importance God places on praise this way: "He does so not because He is an egotist with selfish desires, but because He has our best interests at heart. Praise and thanksgiving help us rise above self-centeredness to Christ-centeredness."

Indeed, the feeling of helplessness seems to me to be a crossroads in the process of crisis where many Christians make a decision to resent their own impotence or, with relief, to turn over responsibility to God. As I look back at my experience with Celeste's tumor, I recognize that the helpless feeling was preceded by other emotions: shock and unsureness, a fascination with the potential danger, a time of panic, a feeling of testing and pushing against the limits of the situation. When I finally understood that I had done all that I could do that would help her, then the feeling of helplessness settled in. The feeling was brief. Because I know me (and I'm not much, so to speak), the thought that God would take care of the situation was like a reprieve to me.

At that time many well-meaning people advised me, "Just live a day at a time," and I found that this was good counsel when amended by *Decision* magazine writer Carol Wilson: "Only one day at a time; only one Person to please." Through praise in prayer we leave this earthly situation and are able to join God in a different setting. Psalm 100:4, in fact, speaks of praise as the medium through which we enter God's courts, and I have the mental image of my praise—my acknowledgment of who God is and what He has done in the past to reveal Himself—being like a key, a way of accessing His presence. My words take on greater weight, it seems to me, when I think of them not only echoing in the ears of God, but also being heard by the creatures and saints who surround His throne. (Quite often I have stopped in midprayer, stunned by the realization that there are other beings in His presence who, too, might hear what I am asking for in prayer. Sometimes this really helps me objectively evaluate the importance of my requests.)

Is thinking of ourselves in heaven while there is chaos going on around us just escapism? Certainly, if we are neglectful of our responsibilities, it could become such. But there are other advantages besides the peace that being at least temporarily removed from crisis brings.

First of all, visualizing ourselves in heaven will certainly make the eventual transition there easier, more a reunion than a relocation. But there is a more immediate advantage: it changes our view of things here while we wait. One way I have used that visualizing with my son, Ryan, is when he and I are having a discussion about activities in which I will or will not allow him to participate. (Such a conversation with an intelligent, verbal, strong-willed child qualifies in my book as at least a minor crisis.)

Several times I have invited him to "dream" with me about what heaven will be like. We muse about all the happiness and peace there, and then I remind him that in heaven we will remember our earthly relationship of mother and son, but this relationship will exist in our memories, for in heaven we will stand before God's throne as two adult souls. I will have to be able to explain both to him and to God why I raised him the way I did. Such a picture helps Ryan to understand a lot of things.

Having a "heaven mentality" can help any of us when we are in situations beyond our control. "Entering His gates with praise" is indeed a key to His presence, because when we acknowledge His qualities, His acts of greatness, we are firmly establishing in our own minds what is dependably true about Him. This is no act of self-hypnosis but the only way we can grasp His "be-ing."

Like the invisible wind, God's presence in our lives (and its relevance to what we are undergoing) is often not detected by being seen, but is only perceived by its results. We know we cannot establish a human-to-human relationship with Him, so we concretize His reality in our own minds by what we do know, do sense, do see—the results of His power, greatness, and goodness in our lives.

In crisis, saints through the ages have depended upon biblical praise and a mindset toward heaven. These concepts bring with them their own joy, their own reward, for praise, as C. S. Lewis observed, "is the mode of love which always has some element of joy in it." We see this in Paul and Silas, sitting at midnight with bleeding backs in a rancid prisonhole, singing praise to their God. That was because Paul was going through a process, learning what he would later call a "secret" in Philippians 4:12. This was not a catechism-type instruction, but the kind of indoctrination, *mueo* in Greek, that those of his time who were inducted into secret societies received. This was like a password, a felt and perceived knowing rather than a transmitted body of knowledge. What was the secret? Being content.

This same contentment and confidence in the God who allowed Paul to do all things through Him—this same contentment marked the men and women who throughout history died, as the song says, "for truth and Jesus' lovely name." It has been true of saints through to our own age. To me the supreme example of biblical praise in our own time has always been Betsie ten Boom, the sister of Corrie ten Boom, who even in a Nazi prison camp could praise God for such things as having to be strip-searched (it helped her identify with Jesus who had undergone similar humiliation) and fleas (which later enabled her to have Bible studies uninterrupted by guards).

What all these praising people in history had in common is the fact that what they were praising bore little resemblance to their surroundings. Nowhere is this more evident than in the wonderful praise passage found in Jonah chapter 2. Here Jonah spoke of how God answered his call of distress. He described the horrifying experience of being in the sea, and then concluded by saying, "You brought my life up from the pit, O Lord my God." His praise is touching, not only because of its fervency, but even more so because of the fact that when he spoke these praise-words to God he was not safely on shore, but was still within the belly of the great fish.

Jonah's example goes far beyond the world's concept of "psyching yourself up" to handle a bad situation. Like Jonah, we in prayer create a world that doesn't exist and then invite God to make it a reality. Believing in something that has not happened is not fantasizing in a way that is opposed to the principles of reality and Christianity. Indeed, such a belief is a godly attribute, for it is God Himself who "calls those things that are not as though they were" (Romans 4:17).

What a great safeguard to such assurance, though, is knowledge of God's nature. We are greatly protected from the dangers that would accost our absolute belief in God's obligation to fulfill any dream we manufacture. Like Shadrach, Meshach, and Abednego in Daniel 3, we can confidently affirm God's ability to save us from any blazing furnace of disaster while simultaneously admitting that He can take any course of action (including no discernible action) He chooses. Knowing that all the while He will be doing the best, the most loving thing He can for us will help us, like those three young men, to keep our position of faithfulness to Him firm, regardless of whether He answers our request or not.

Indeed, it takes no stretch of faith to believe in an entity who invariably does just what you say. Such things do exist. They are called robots.

The concept of a manageable and tractable God is far removed from truth. In acknowledging who the true God is and what He has done in the past, we acknowledge also how unlike us He is, how dissimilar His actions and reactions to ours. Where the world judges reality by what it can see and touch, God invites us to see beyond that, telling us that "hope that is seen is no hope at all" (Romans 8:24). He is not a God who "goes with the flow" of this world, for its every current is—apart from Him—hurtful to us. As we remember the greatness of His past wondrous works, we must remind ourselves that His greatness was all the more visible because it contrasted with the bad circumstances it overcame.

Very rarely can we have a complete freedom of choice over all our circumstances. And so we come full circle, back to Frankl's concept of the freedom to choose our attitudes. We choose to praise or not to praise. We choose to improve praise as we do any other spiritual skill— by meditation, learning, practice—or we choose to let it die unspoken within us. We choose to let it be a part of our life that other people can "catch" from us, or we quarantine ourselves and our faith.

Today, and each day I approach God in prayer, I can use the key of biblical praise to enter into that special court and commune with my God. I can tell Him that I will love Him and trust Him no matter what happens in my life, because He has always proven Himself faithful, and He will not change.

There, in that prayer-sanctuary behind the curtain described in Hebrews 6:19-20, I can meet my Lord, for He is waiting there for me, prepared to be my advocate. He draws the cherubim-embroidered curtain of blue and purple and crimson across the scenes of doubt and confusion I leave behind me in my physical surroundings. As I visualize Him beside me, I gain strength just from the thought of His presence.

But there is another guest there, a presence that followed Jesus into the sanctuary.

That guest is hope, which the Hebrew writer described as an anchor for the soul. It has preceded every Christian with even the most fainthearted request who has approached that curtain.

Unseen but real, sometimes weak in my life, it nonetheless waits there in my prayer-place, too, and invites me to dream great dreams for the future—lovingly superintended by a powerful God who wants only the best for me.

PART TWO

Praise and Prayer in Multiple/Sustained Crises

During the course of writing this book on crisis, which had as its focal experience the time three years before when Celeste suffered from the skull tumor, my life underwent some dramatic developments. Within the span of four weeks, both my mother and Celeste barely escaped death.

Writing a book on crisis was replaced with living through multiple crises. Many of my Christian friends commented on God's timing, and I responded that perhaps He was giving me some on-the-job training for writing the book. (My son, Ryan, suggested that if that was true, he wanted me next to write a book on getting rich.)

I learned that the principles of praise that I had codified for myself through Celeste's tumor experience were still valid, but harder to live out in everyday life when they had to be consciously applied on a long-term or repeated basis. I know this is one of the lessons God wanted me to learn so that I would not be Pollyannaish in passing on this information to others.

On the one hand, I have been sobered by this second set of experiences. The weight of the situation came home to me one day recently when my friend Carol Norris, a photographer living in Colorado Springs, called to ask when I wanted to set up an appointment to come for a visit and the three-generation portrait of Mother, myself, and Celeste that we had discussed. I realized that, but for God's mercy, no such picture would have been possible.

I have been sobered, but also greatly encouraged by the reaffirmation that God is indeed unchangingly loving, in good times as well as bad, in short crises as well as those that seemingly have no end.

He is strong. He is loving.

ICU (MOTHER)

Thus we do penance,
We the sons and daughters
Who wait in these glassed-in
Naves and apses of our fear

We dent our forearms, leaning on the
Bedrail altarrails
And pray for atonement
Through our own stiffened legs
And numbed hands
That stroke, stroke

And we recite our inward litany of neglects, small
And large, that we must
Memorize; they must
Be recorded so that we
Can properly repent

We barter like Hannahs,
Beg like Hezekiahs,
Negotiate like Abrahams

And like Magdalenes awakened
In the predawn Easter darkness

We wait.
We wait.

CAT SCAN (CELESTE)

Child of my body, how still you lie
In this, the haven of your pain,
The sleep where you are sheltered
Beneath your eyelids

Even your blood is your foe now
Should it marshal and clot
In the rush to repair all this hurting

You enter this machine,
This ring of lights,
As serenely as the dawn.

Child of my body—
How still you lie.

SIX

The Rubber Meets the Road

May 9, 1988 began as a beautiful, sunny day. The breath of spring was fragrant with promise and I entered this Monday with a firm agenda.

I had arisen early, showered, made the children's lunches, had our traditional devotional and prayer time. After they left for school, our dog, Ebony, and I walked to a nearby bank, where I made a deposit and then returned home again.

I was still in my walking clothes and paint-spattered jogging shoes, sitting at my computer writing when just before ten o'clock the telephone rang. My answering machine delivered its obligatory message, and then I heard my mother's voice.

"Latayne, pick up the phone." I obeyed.

"Something's wrong. I'm so dizzy I can't even stand up." I considered the blinking cursor on my computer screen, the Spanish class I was to teach at 1:00, my own worn jeans and shoes.

"Well, how about I change and I'll come over. Do you think I need to take you to the doctor. . .?" My mumbling was interrupted by a moan from her. "I'll be right there. I'm leaving now."

I grabbed my Spanish class materials and heaved them into the back seat of my car as over my shoulder I told the workmen who were painting the outside of our house that I expected to be back in a couple of hours.

Mother's house is only a few minutes from mine. I drove into her driveway and opened the door of my car. There was an odd sound outside that I could not identify. It was rhythmic and low, like the guttural sound of a reluctant car engine being coaxed into action on a cold morning.

I looked around for its source. It was coming from my mother.

She was sitting on a bench on her front porch, slumped over to one side, vomiting. In one hand were her keys—she had had the presence of mind to stumble outside and open her iron gate before collapsing there. The fact that she had last week borrowed my key to her gate to make an extra copy flickered through my mind as I opened the otherwise impregnable gate.

One look at her unfocusing eyes confirmed my fears. I squatted down beside her.

"Mother, I'm here. Can you let me help you into the car so I can get you to a doctor?"

She shook her head. "Too dizzy."

I looked at her bulk—well over 200 pounds—and knew that I could not possibly carry her to the car.

"I'm calling an ambulance."

The next few minutes were spent running back and forth from the phone to the porch; calling the ambulance, her doctor, my husband; finding her purse and health-insurance card and bottles of prescription drugs.

The ride to the hospital in the ambulance increased my fears as I heard the paramedics call ahead to the hospital to report her steadily rising blood pressure and pulse. As soon as she was admitted to the emergency room, several preliminary tests were begun. The nurse who had taken the artery blood for blood-gas tests was called out of the room suddenly, and she asked me to hold a gauze pad on the still-bleeding spot on Mother's wrist.

"I'll be right back," the nurse assured me. "I'll be in the next room—there's an accident victim who's just been admitted and they need some help. If anything happens, you just yell for me."

I nodded, grateful for the chance to relieve my helpless feeling by doing something. As Mother drifted in and out of consciousness, I was alone in the room, which was silent except for her labored breathing and the sound of the monitor, which showed with jagged lines and brisk blips just how hard her heart was working.

At first I thought it was my imagination—that the blips were coming closer together. Soon they seemed almost frantic to my ears. I stared in near-fascination at the coursing lines, then tore myself away to call outside the door for the nurse.

No sooner had I turned back to the monitor than the blips suddenly stopped.

The line on the monitor went flat.

The bedlam of the following events was nightmarish—nurses shouting for assistance, the urgent paging for a cardiologist, white-gowned people who appeared out of nowhere with machines to shock her heart back into beating. The air was filled with phrases I could not understand, and others I could not accept.

"Third degree heart blockage."

"No pulse."

"Get Dr. Kroke—stat."

Someone asking me if I was a relative, could give permission for a temporary pacemaker to be installed. Someone else pushing me out of the room, out of the way.

The terrible agony of being alone among all those people who surrounded my mother's lifeless body.

The urgent soothings of a passing nurse who relayed information to my husband, Dan. The receiver hanging from the lobby pay phone, dropped by Dan when the commotion began.

Groans that came from within me, that sounded like they were coming from someone else.

Fast-swinging doors and the arrival of my two brothers, breathing fear.

The words from Dr. Sears, Mother's internist, delivered like a solemn sermon inside the hospital chapel: "Your mother's very ill and may die. She's had a serious stroke and her heart had stopped but is now beating again."

The reprise: twenty-four hours will tell, twenty-four hours will tell, twenty-four hours . . .

How wan she looked on those light-bleached sheets of the ICU, how vulnerable. The wires from the temporary pacemaker protruded from her collarbone, attaching her to her landscape of machines and tubes. One eye flickered uncontrollably; the other was filled with apprehension as she sought assurance from us, her children, but couldn't hear, was too weary to listen. Nurses silently took vital signs, patting our shoulders as they left.

It was nearly midnight when the last of my friends from church left the ICU lounge. I took off the jogging shoes and wondered how many of the people who had come today had thought what one friend did: that the paint on them was blood. No wonder so many people had stared at my shoes.

The ICU nurse assigned to Mother that night gave me sheets and blankets for the couch in the lounge and assured me that he would help me keep my promise to Mother—that I would come anytime she needed me in the night. But my sleep was so deep that it took a while for me to understand what he was saying as he shook my shoulder three hours later.

A new enemy had surfaced—a paralysis of the left side of her body. She was more awake and very afraid. I spent the rest of the night at her side, holding her hand, watching her rouse and look for me through half-opened eyes that soon closed again. The night was a collage of prayer and fears and wonderings about all the unasked questions about her relationship with God. By dawn the paralysis was fading and she began to relax.

I decided to go to the hospital cafeteria to eat something to stop the grinding feeling in my stomach. But my brief feelings of optimism fled when I returned. Mother had experienced another "episode," as the nurse termed it. The pacemaker had not functioned; her heart had stopped again. But by some providential timing, the cardiologist was standing just outside her door and was able, once again, to revive her. The first time I had left her—and now as I returned, she lay unconscious again, twice-spared, but spent.

A new pacemaker was installed, and this last stopping of her heart was the turning point after which she continued gradually to improve over the week that she spent in the hospital. Scores of friends from church kept me company, and as she improved, so did my spirits. There were even times to laugh. One day I was sitting in the ICU waiting room and struck up a conversation with another woman there. I remarked on the humor of the fact that the man who had twice revived my mother was named Dr. Kroke.

"Oh, I know Dr. Kroke," she replied. "He assisted on my husband's heart surgery."

"Oh, who did the surgery?" I asked, just to further the conversation.

"Dr. Slash and Dr. Moneymaker," she innocently replied. Mother's sense of humor, too, returned with her health. It wasn't too long before she was trying to figure out how to run a bedpan with money in it down a wire to the hamburger joint across the street to supplement the gruel and gelatin she was served.

From the very beginning, she was aware that God had spared her life so that she could make some needed changes in her relationship to Him. She regarded this as pure grace; and today, fifty-four pounds lighter, blood pressure normal, she would say that the stroke was perhaps the only way God could have gotten her attention to make her take charge of her health.

She spent the second week after her stroke recovering at my house, where we both learned a lot about cholesterol and low-fat foods. We were also able to spend leisurely time discussing our individual relationships to God. For the first time in my life, my mother is actively involved in regular church attendance. In fact, she even quoted Scripture to me the other day—something even a year ago I would have regarded as impossible.

The next two weeks of my life are a blur—having spent two weeks with my mother, I had a lot of catching up to do with household affairs, study, and all the activities that crowd the calendar at the end of the school year.

Monday, June 6, marked the four-week anniversary of Mother's stroke. It was the first day of summer vacation too, and Ryan and Celeste and I had a long list of things we wanted to do. We arose early and took my mother-in-law to the airport. Then the children and I picked up Ryan's friend Stephen and went swimming and then delivered graduation gifts. In the afternoon we ran errands and went to a friend's house and picked cherries for a couple of hours. I delivered Celeste to a birthday slumber party at a friend's grandmother's house, then Ryan and I returned home. Dan and I pitted, bagged, and froze the cherries we'd picked, and I made a pie. When I finally sank exhausted into bed after ten o'clock, I remarked to Dan that I couldn't remember a time in my life when I had been more tired.

Just moments later the phone rang. Dan answered it.

"It's somebody saying something about Celeste," he said, handing the phone to me.

The voice on the phone was quivering. It was the grandmother at the slumber party.

"Latayne, Celeste has fallen—we can't get her to wake up," she said.

"I'll be right there," I said. I don't know why I didn't ask any questions. We awakened Ryan and his friend Stephen who was spending the night, and all put back on the first clothes we found, spattered with sweet, red cherry juice.

Dan raced the car at nearly eighty miles an hour up the road to the house where Celeste was, about five miles away. As we neared the final intersection, an ambulance screamed through it, lights flashing. We turned and followed it, our hearts sinking as it stopped in front of our destination. A city paramedic truck was already there.

Neighbors and birthday guests were in the yard, throughout the house, with solemn searching looks as we pushed through to the backyard. There, on a concrete slab, Celeste lay face-down and motionless, her face resting on her folded arm.

The questions of the paramedics, the chatter of pre-teenage girls who wanted to explain, the hostess's grief-stricken face—all these receded when Celeste stirred. The paramedics were concerned with a neck injury, for there was no blood and no visible sign of a head injury.

The story came out—all the children had been out in the yard, jumping from a short brick wall and swinging on a long tarzan-rope that was suspended from a nearby tree. The first time Celeste had tried it, she had scraped her shin as she swung back to the brick retaining wall. She waited a second turn. But this time when the rope completed its arc, it snapped and she fell, slamming her head directly (and audibly) into the brick wall.

There she had remained, crumpled and unconscious, until the children had dragged her over to the porch slab.

When the paramedics were able to rouse her from her stupor, her eyes were wild, like those of a sleepwalker. She would try to answer questions, but would doze off. Only when they brought out a backboard and began to strap her into it did she respond. As they tightened the straps over her head to transport her to the ambulance, she fought them, screaming.

My sweet, passive Celeste who would let a doctor cut into her scalp without hesitation, the obedient child whose greatest fear was not hurt, but hurting the feelings of others—clawed at the straps and writhed.

"You don't understand," she said, her speech slurred with pain and emotion, "I've got a headache!" Only her daddy could convince her to lie still as she was lifted into the ambulance, and he joined her there for the ride.

Ryan and Stephen were silent in the back seat of the car as we followed the ambulance to the hospital. Ryan was still dealing with the rage he felt at what he thought he had seen—the paramedics hurting his sister.

My feelings were not nearly as focused. The sight of the ambulance in front of me brought to the surface many emotions as I considered that it held not an anonymous stranger but my daughter.

I understood what a head or neck injury could mean. I understood that it could mean paralysis or other physical damage. Worse yet, it could mean that her mind could be impaired. I thought of how, just the week before, she had stood tall and radiant at her violin concert. I thought of her distress at the first B to mar her straight-A report cards. I remembered her sweet, loving nature.

This is crisis, I thought. The book I am writing—what I've been telling people—does it work in real life? Can a normal everyday Christian like me really praise in a situation like this?

Oh, yes!

For God is good. He is a good God. He loves Celeste much more than I do. He has always done what was best in my life for me. He would, I was sure, do what was best now.

What a relief I felt! The situation had not changed—but then, again, neither had the God who was controlling it! I knew could face the specters that would haunt me—the fear of physical damage, the fear that her mind or emotions might be marred. I forced myself to imagine the worst thing of all. I knew the worst would not be death, for she was a Christian. So I made myself visualize her immobilized, unable to feed herself, unable to communicate. I thought of her in this state through her teenage years, into adulthood.

Then I promised God that I would love her and serve her, no matter what, for the rest of her life. And I promised Him that I would love Him and serve Him for the rest of my life—no matter what.

By the time we arrived at the hospital, I was anxious only with the impatience I felt in wanting to know a diagnosis. God Himself, I knew, would be taking care of all the details behind the scene. I just wanted to know what to call it.

The emergency room physician, Dr. Wilkie, was soothing. "I've had my own son in here on this same table three times with bumps on the head," he said. "And he's only five years old!"

We explained to him Celeste's previous history, including her eosinophilic granuloma tumor, as he examined her.

"I think she has a concussion," he said, "but I can't find the goose egg. Just to be on the safe side, considering her skull surgery, we'll run her through a quick CAT scan." He looked at our faces. "And don't worry! You'll have your little sleepyhead home in another hour."

I hurried out to the waiting room to give Ryan and Stephen the good news. Since it was by now after midnight, even the delicious freedom of getting to watch late-night television was wearing thin for them. Instead, they had turned to talking about Celeste's condition. They listened while I told them what the doctor had said, and then they began to tell me how they'd encouraged each other with all the examples of God's providence in the situation—the ambulance had gotten there quickly, Celeste was regaining consciousness, the hospital was nearby.

I hurried back into the room, because Celeste had begun vomiting. She was taken down the hall to the laboratory.

The doctor returned—but with little of his former cheer. He would not meet our eyes and quickly left. The minutes dragged on to nearly an hour.

Dan was trying to hold in his emotions, but the delay made it harder and harder for him. He paced, trying not to cry.

During the time of Celeste's tumor, he had gone several days without being able to speak to anyone without weeping. I had been the solid one, and he had depended on me. But he had resolved to be stronger in any future crises; and indeed, he had been a great support to me during my mother's illness. But here he was again, unable to endure the pain he was feeling.

I put my arms around him. "You can cry if you want to," I assured him. "You don't have to handle things the way I do. And I'm really sorry if in the past I've made you feel bad for breaking down. You can go ahead and feel and do whatever you need to."

Our tears together there were as potent as any medicine in that hospital. By the time the doctor returned with the CAT scan pictures, we were prepared for what he had to tell us.

When Celeste's head hit that brick wall, it struck solidly on the side of her skull. That is why there was no single "bump." The scan picture showed a long fracture from the top of her head all the way to the base of her skull. Another fracture transversed it, extending several inches to the side. Apparently there was another fracture behind the opposite ear, because blood had leaked behind it.

When I went into the waiting room to tell the boys, they had again been spending their time encouraging one another with all the ways that God had taken care of Celeste. Wasn't it good, they now reasoned, that God used Celeste's old granuloma experience to cause the doctor to do the CAT scan when he thought this was just a minor injury? Wasn't it great that the doctor had children so he could be understanding? Wasn't God's timing terrific, letting this happen when school was out so she wouldn't have to make up lessons?

I walked back into the examining room, humbled by their faith and by the overt and natural way they had found to praise God.

A neurosurgeon, Dr. Hal Hankinson, was called in, and he advised that Celeste be transferred to a larger hospital with fuller facilities. She had one more ambulance ride ahead of her that night.

Celeste spent a week in that hospital. During that time, there were times when her blood pressure dropped so dangerously low that the nurses suspected internal bleeding. The CAT scan showed spots of blood all over the surface of her brain, mute testimony to the force of the impact of her fall. The swelling of her brain was treated with steroids, and because of the intense pain, she was given the same kind of medicine, according to the nurses, that was given to terminal cancer patients.

Though she was not conscious most of the time, she had many visitors and well-wishers. In fact, there were so many helium-filled balloons in her hospital room that the nurses joked about running out of ceiling space.

When she did become lucid, she was very curious about what had happened to her. She had no memory of the fall, nor the events of the hours that preceded and followed it. She listened gravely as I tried to explain what it meant to have multiple skull fractures, a concussion, cerebral contusions, intracerebral hemorrhage.

She turned her small face away from me.

"What's the matter?" I asked.

"Oh, Mom . . ." She choked with emotion, unable to finish.

"Just tell me, darling. What is it?"

"Well," she blubbered, "I just want to know one thing. Does this, um, mean I'm going to be stupid?"

I gathered her into my arms, laughing with relief. "The fact that you're able to ask that question, Celeste, means that you are not going to be stupid!" I felt her relaxing in my arms, soon laughing too.

By the end of her week's stay in the hospital, Celeste was ready to return home, where she spent another quiet week continuing her recovery.

Now several months after her fall, she has returned to a fairly normal lifestyle. Because of some apparent tearing of the olfactory nerve when she hit that wall, she has lost most of her sense of smell, and what she can smell is odd or unfamiliar to her. She has headaches that are frequent and painful. Frequently she experiences sudden dizzy spells, and we have been warned by her neurosurgeon to watch for seizures. Even a recent hit in the head with a basketball sent us back through the hierarchy of doctors and to the CAT scan: the nerve scars left from her previous concussion make even schoolyard collisions unbearably painful.

Like many other events of relatively short duration, the fall may affect her for the rest of her life on this earth. She has accepted all these things with great courage and faith.

Not too long ago she and I were talking together about her concussion and the effect it has had on all our lives. She asked me, "Mom, why do you think God let that happen to me?"

Her question is one that is bound to occur to anyone who undergoes an experience like hers. My answer to her was in three parts.

First of all, I told her that God did indeed "let" it happen, not because He wanted to punish her for anything, but because He does not step in and prevent bad things in all cases in people's lives. If He did, then we would never make mistakes, never sin, never learn—and have no need for a Savior.

Second, because He did not prevent it does not mean that He did not know it was going to happen. In fact, I told Celeste, that as soon as she began growing inside of me, God not only knew about this coming accident, but I believe that He was also making provision to lessen its bad effects on her. I reminded her of Romans 8:28, which says that God makes all things work together for good for those who love Him.

Third, the most important word in Celeste's question, though, was not the "why," it was the "me." It is easy to "explain" God's role in the lives of others when they are facing crisis. It is much harder to reason why such things have settled onto me.

I returned to Romans 8:28. "Celeste, angel, perhaps this fall happened to you because God knew what a good example of Christ you would be to others. He knew you would still love Him even in bad times."

She was silent for quite a long time as she considered this. Then, with a tiny smile on her lips, she answered.

"Yeah, Mom, you're right."

No pridefulness at acknowledging her faith, no resentment of the God who controls her life.

How much I am learning about how to be a Christian.

So I span this pain:
Mother to my daughter,
Daughter to my mother:

As they have suffered
I become the connecting link
Where the fires do not
Actually burn, but where
The singeing takes place;
The charring of the
Handle that joins two
Hurts

SEVEN

Dealing with the Aftermath of Sustained Crisis

Recently my twelve-year-old son, Ryan, returned home from Camp Blue Haven, where he spent a wonderful two weeks learning about the Lord—and about some other things, as well. A couple of days after he arrived at home, I noticed a large, angry-looking wound on the back of his right hand.

"Ryan, how did you get that scrape on your hand?" I asked, holding his hand up for a little closer look.

"Oh, Mom . . ." He looked embarrassed—the look that I am beginning to associate with the subject of girls. "It was just a game," he said awkwardly.

"A game?" I was incredulous, unable to connect this injury with anything I think of as fun.

"Well, see, a girl came up to me at camp and while everyone else was watching, she told me to give her my hand and turn away," he began. Apparently, she challenged Ryan to keep his hand out of view while she gently rubbed the thin skin on the back of his hand with her fingernail. The continued abrasion had two effects: it deadened the skin and little by little wore away its outside layer. When, several minutes later, she released his hand, it was bloodied. He couldn't very well protest—after all, it had not hurt, and many of the onlookers had been in on the ruse and were watching him closely for any "unmanly" reaction.

How like the effect of sustained crisis on souls that little episode is! So many times we are completely unaware of the effect of repeated or sustained assaults on our well-being. We can notice the numbing effect that in many ways holds us together and protects us while we are dealing directly with crisis, and we appreciate the occasional feelings of distance that allow us to cope. Sometimes this numbness, though, can spill over into other areas of our lives or live on even when a crisis is past and prevent us from completely feeling some of the emotions we must experience for our own healing.

Christians are especially like my son, Ryan, too, in that we are often being closely watched, not only by non-Christians who appraise God by how His followers act under pressure, but also by other Christians who depend upon us in other ways. When we who have suffered finally see our own injuries that are a by-product of crisis, we who have been "strong" may be ashamed to ask for help when the situation itself seems under control.

Sustained crisis always takes its toll. While I was inwardly thanking the Lord for His help during my mother's stroke and Celeste's injury, I was also congratulating myself on the fact that my blood pressure and pulse were staying steady. These are important barometers of my health because I have a family history of heart attacks and strokes. But weeks of all-night vigils in the hospital combined with watching slow recoveries did have an effect. My menstrual cycle became a disconcerted noncycle that resulted in minor surgery for me a few weeks after Celeste's fall; and then there was the subsequent diagnosis of another stress-related condition: my body temperature rose over a degree and remained that way for many years.

Do these things mean that I was not completely trusting God? Are they an indication of an inner battle over my feelings about these crises, one that is unresolved and thus ongoing?

Of course, I must admit the possibility of the truth of such ideas. I am not perfect in any area of my life; certainly I have room to grow in trusting God in crisis. But I can look inside myself and honestly admit before God that I have no outstanding doubts about His nature, nor His intention to bless me, now and for the rest of my life.

The conclusion I have come to is that all growth has a price. Even if the only residual effect of a crisis is that it sobers us and our view of life on this earth, this effect itself is at the expense of our former frivolity and lightheartedness. Such a new attitude can be mourned over, or it can be used as a tool.

Even "bad" effects of a crisis can be used as tools, too—my failing health reminds me not only of my own mortality, but also of the fact that my body is a gift from God over which I have stewardship, not ownership. I can see many far-reaching effects of my own experience with sustained crisis more clearly the farther time separates me from it. For instance, I can look back and see this experience in "stages," whereas at the time that each phase was materializing, I was only aware of one more crisis. For that reason, I do not believe that anyone while in the midst of crisis can distinguish between a single crisis and a sustained crisis. All crisis is by definition sustained: all crisis seems open-ended when it is happening.

Nonetheless, when one crisis follows close on the heels of another, it becomes obvious that each has its own flavor. Like stairstep-children, each with a different personality in spite of a common font, clustered crises must be dealt with on an individual basis. The same rules apply, but sometimes with varying applications. For instance, I was equally able to believe that God was in control with Mother's stroke as with Celeste's fall. I concluded in both cases that since God had been a powerful advocate in the past for anyone who trusted Him, that He would certainly aid me when I depended on Him.

The peace-bordering-on-joy I felt after Celeste's ambulance trip was only distantly related to the stunned acceptance I felt of Mother's illness. In both cases I could acknowledge that God would do the very best thing possible. But while I was confidently assured of Celeste's spiritual condition, I had no such confidence in Mother's, for before that time she had never shared with me whether or not she believed she was saved.

In the case of both my mother and Celeste, I wanted them to live! But with Mother, it went further—I couldn't bear the thought of her dying without us both knowing that she would spend eternity in heaven, with Christ—and with me.

Yes, I kept all those whispered promises to God to speak to her about her soul. The fact that He granted her, and me, the time to gain the assurance we both needed, is a demonstration of unalloyed grace.

Thus God used my greatest fears to precipitate great growth. This mirrors something that a counselor friend of mine, Paula Huguley, pointed out recently to me: the Chinese word-symbol for crisis is a combination of the symbol for danger and the symbol for opportunity. If we try to ignore the danger, we run the risk of becoming either flippant or numb. But if we disparage the opportunity, we pillage our own dearly bought assets.

One of these expensive assets is our new awareness of God's role in our lives. Once we get past the point of correctly assessing who He is, we soon come to the conclusion that He inherently has the ability to do an infinite number of things to affect or change the situation we are in. And let's be realistic—the question is not so much "What is God capable of doing here?" but rather "What is He *going to do* to help me right now?" We all want to be believers in miracles when we desperately need one.

We have already dealt with the very real danger of misjudging God either before or in the midst of crisis. But there is another danger that is just as chilling—that of misjudging ourselves. This danger has two faces: the first is the pride that can result when God answers our prayers, and the other face is guilt.

Let's look at pride first. It probably has not escaped your notice that each crisis I faced that I related in this book has turned out well. Celeste and my mother are both well, physically and spiritually, and I have drawn a direct connection between their crises and the role of praise in my own life. Yet all around us are good, godly people who have faced similar crises who arise every morning to an ownerless teddy bear and an empty place at the breakfast table, or who will for the rest of their lives buy funeral wreaths instead of cards on Mother's Day.

Does having my mother and my daughter alive mean that because Latayne Scott learned how to praise I somehow staved off disaster with this knowledge? A couple of years ago I faced this question when I presented a seminar on prayer where I related how important prayer was to me during Celeste's tumor experience. The other speaker on the program was Pam Nicholas, a deeply spiritual young woman whose only child, Rachel, died of an incurable disease after only five short months of life. Was my praise "better" than hers? Does God love my family more than her and her grieving husband?

I have wrestled with these torturing thoughts and with my own certain knowledge that Pam is at least as close, if not closer, to God than I am. In thinking about it, I have come to the conclusion that there is indeed a direct connection between praise and my crisis experiences, as the previous chapters of this book have shown. But I have drawn great comfort from knowing that for me (and Pam and thousands of other Christians), praise was never intended to be thought of as a way of controlling the situation; *it was a way to allow God to control me.*

My acknowledgment that He is God, that He has shown Himself to be strong and loving in the past—this did not obligate Him to any certain course of action for me. In fact, when I left the emergency room cubicle where there was a flat line on my mother's heart monitor, there was a period of time in which I believed her to be dead. Even in the midst of the stunning feelings of horror and grief and loss was the superintending thought: He is still God, and He knows what He is doing.

Because my mother is older than I am, there will probably come a day in my life when I will stand by her bedside and there will be no dramatic resuscitation. I don't expect to live the rest of my life and not face the specter of death, either my own or that of those I love. (As my husband, who sells life insurance says, the statistics on dying are still a hundred percent—everyone will die.) And Christians are not exempt from these statistics, nor their effects on the lives of those of us who survive.

Thus I can take no credit, impute myself no merit for the decision of my sovereign God to spare the lives of Mother and Celeste; for surely in the future He will require of them what He had earlier declined.

The second danger of misjudging ourselves is that of taking on ourselves a load of guilt. Of course, if a crisis has been precipitated by our own willful disobedience or negligence, feeling guilty is appropriate, at least up to the point where it brings us to repentance and a resultant change in future behavior. But crises, especially those that involve the life and death of loved ones, rarely are brought about by our own actions.

We may know that in our minds, but our hearts tell us differently when we are sitting at the bedside of someone we love.

I clearly remember the first afternoon that I came home from the hospital after Celeste's fall. I took off the clothes I had worn the previous day, slept in, and worn again. After a shower, I dressed and went out into our backyard and rested in the hammock. The cicadas were buzzing loudly and the sun filtered in sheets through the leaves of the mulberry and cypress trees that supported the hammock.

My mind was reeling. First Mother's brush with death, and now Celeste, who had already suffered so much. What, I wondered, did the proximity of these two events mean? Why were the two females I loved most in this life allowed to undergo these things? What did they have in common?

The answer was automatic. What they had in common was me.

For the first time, I saw the focus of these crises to be not the individuals who were most affected, but myself. Knowing that God is not arbitrary in the timing of events I began to search my heart for whatever causes I could find there—causes for the suffering of these two people I loved. Was I so stubborn, I wondered, that God could only get through to me by making the people I loved suffer?

There in that hammock, I felt the allure of the arms of a lover reaching for me, a lover whose first advances satisfy those of us who are suffering; yet a lover whose embrace crushes and kills and drains. That lover is guilt.

When no one else can give us answers, he has the one explanation that always fits every situation. We listen eagerly to his reasoning, which has nothing to do with logic, yet somehow we find satisfaction in his whispered rationale that we somehow caused the situation; or if not, that we should have been able to foresee and forestall it.

He wears the mask of responsibility and accountability and maturity, a mask that can melt onto his face until we are powerless to distinguish him from his disguise.

Sometimes he must be unmasked by someone outside our situation telling us verbally, "This was not your fault." But the longer we lie in his arms, the stronger his power becomes over us.

His attraction at that moment was overwhelming. But his strength faded as I considered the fact even logic assures me that God does not hold me accountable for the rupture of a blood vessel in my mother's brain, nor for the weakened rope that broke under Celeste's weight.

Yet now so many of us live with the consequences of these things. On the one hand, I am assured of absolution of guilt for them. But on the other hand, I dare not overlook the lessons God intends for me to learn from two near-tragedies that uprooted my life, four weeks apart.

Even a considerable amount of time later I cannot answer those ongoing questions completely to my own satisfaction. They have become a legacy, the paradigm of a fingernail's constant rubbing on the back of my soul's hand: sustained crisis, the summer of 1988.

UNBORN CHILDREN
(FOR MY SON RYAN)

This writhing inside me entreats in silence,
Groping for words through lips that have never spoken.
Child of few yesterdays and all tomorrows:
Through the muffled stillness of the waters,
Only the echo of my blood rushes through
Hollowing chambers to you.

("Eye hath not seen, nor ear heard . . . "
And yet, I know you.
Why can you not speak as I speak?
Will your love ever match Mine?
Will the light of birth open
Your unused eyes to my yearning?)

I, too, move restlessly through terrestrial waters
As conscious of self as a child,
Struggling against a mercantile world. Above, a
Father waits for me
Reaching through beating waves of sound
And senselessness;
Patiently waiting for me to
See as I have been seen, to
Know as I am known;
Wanting me to
Push my way out of this dark world-womb
Into His light.
(1975)

EIGHT
The Relationship of Praise to Prayer

Recently I was asked to present a seminar on the subject of praise. Many people put in many hours sending out invitations, arranging publicity, preparing food and decorations.

Anticipation was in the air as the auditorium began to fill. I looked around and noticed that many in the audience were women who I knew had small children. These women had obviously arranged babysitters and were anxious to use these hours of "freedom" (I reflected as I remembered my days as a young mother) in a way that maximized the time. I was humbled by the realization that every person there, in fact, had chosen to spend this Saturday learning about praise instead of any number of other ways the time could have been spent.

After I was introduced, I mounted the platform with my notes hidden in a single book. It was *The Hallelujah Factor*, a book that I knew many of these women had studied.

"You know," I began, "this has been a really rough time for me. I didn't sleep well last night—there was a dog barking that kept me awake. When I got up this morning, my contact lenses were just killing me. And the more I thought about it, the less worthy I felt to address all you people about praise.

"But I know that Jack Taylor, who wrote this book, really did some fine research on the subject of praise and so I thought I would share with you some of his thoughts today."

The sympathy in several listeners' eyes was fading. I opened the book and began reading.

"*The Hallelujah Factor*, by Jack Taylor. Page one . . . "

I began to read aloud the first section of the book in a flat, even voice, sneaking glances at the audience, which had turned into a restlessly moving mass. I continued. Many people, especially those who had planned and executed this seminar, were shifting uncomfortably and looking at each other in bewilderment. Even Lita Diaz, one of my most loyal friends, had a glazed look in her eyes as she struggled to listen.

I closed the book.

"You came here to hear about praise, didn't you?"

The movement in the audience stopped.

"Don't you see? How do you think God feels when we come to Him with our excuses about how we just can't 'get in the mood' to praise, and then we offer Him a warmed-over version of someone else's thoughts?" They got the point!

Though I planned this incident to make people aware of the importance of spontaneity and honesty in praise, it points out the importance of another aspect of praise that I have only barely touched on in discussing the role of praise in crisis: praise is not just saying things about God—it includes talking intimately with Him.

But that's a definition of prayer, you might say. Yes, and the connection between praise and prayer becomes more obvious when we consider that the conclusions we come to in praising God (again: acknowledging who He is, what He has done in the past, and concluding from these what He will do for me in the future) are likewise laid bare in how we address Him.

If indeed in praise we appraise God—verbalizing all His strengths and qualities—then the logical conclusion of prayer is an evaluation of ourselves where we clearly see our deficits, our needs, weaknesses, desires, and thus by our asking for these things we establish the nature of our relationship with the God we ask these things of. Another way of saying this is that in praise we list and delineate the qualities that make

God who and what He is. In prayer, we admit that we are none of those things: we are not God.

Though they greatly overlap in many areas, there are several points at which praise and prayer maintain their distinctiveness. The most obvious point is the point of focus. Praise must, of course, look toward God, zeroing in on His qualities and abilities. Prayer certainly must contain praise to be acceptable to God, but when the strictly praise elements are sifted out, prayer tends to focus on me and my needs or, in the case of intercessory prayer, the needs of others. In praise, we acknowledge God. In prayer, we acknowledge our need of Him.

Our distance from God—the knowledge that He is great and we are not—drives us to both praise and prayer. But in no other situation of life is the fact that we are not God more painfully obvious than in crisis. At first, we are stunned and numbed. A natural (but unconscious) reaction is to withdraw and protect ourselves from the onslaught of power that we identify with God, He who is so much above us. The pain of intimacy with Someone upon whom we are totally dependent is sometimes excruciating. Even the comfort of fellowship with Him seems pale in a situation where the stakes are as high as life and death.

Ah, but we need Him too much to withdraw completely. And so we who have in the moments of past tranquility assessed Him to be a loving and powerful God run immediately to the rock of our convictions. No longer do we voice as a creed what we believe of Him; we tell Him to His face. Even those who have no formal introduction to Him will in crisis burst unashamedly into His presence.

It is difficult (and usually invalid) to make any absolute statements about prayer, because prayer, like conversation, varies not only from individual to individual, but also in form, length, intensity, and content as situations change. If this is true in good times, it must be doubly true in bad. In the climax of a crisis, all the "glory words" and magnificents and powerfuls and holies are pushed aside by us as superfluous, for do we not assume all those things of God when we ask Him in desperation, "Help me"? Only later in denouement are we able to do more than that and use this medium of communication to not only ask for specific help, but also to estimate our damages and assets.

When discussing with a friend or a counselor some challenging situation, one which we cannot understand, we sort through facts and try together to find a way of understanding and dealing with it. We may come up with some tentative framework for assessing the situation, but upon discovery of a fact that does not "fit," we may say, "Well, no, that way of looking at this situation couldn't be true because . . ."

So we seek another framework that will accommodate all the facts as we know them. To a Christian, the primary facts beyond all dispute or negotiation are that God knows our situation, understands all its implications and "solutions," and most important, He cares. In prayer we can discuss these things with Him as our friend and counselor, asking for wisdom. He through the Spirit can reveal to us not only what to do, but equally important, how to look at it—God's own perspective on the situation.

In crisis, more than any other time in our lives, we need to see things the way God sees them, for what is before our physical eyes in most cases seems unfair, inequitable, undeserved. (We may give mental assent to certain facts—pain is the result of the willful disobedience of Adam, we are all sinners, the wages of sin is death—but no one can walk as I did beside the stretcher carrying my child and ever consider saying, "Well, yes, she deserves to suffer.")

So how can we have God's perspective? One thing that has been helpful to me is to remember that God does not dwell in our sequential, one-event-follows-another universe. He abides in eternity, where time as we know it does not exist, where past events are just as "present" as our unseen future. If we can trust Him, who sees the outcome of our situation as certainly as He sees our past—and more importantly, trust

Him to use past, present, and future to our advantage as Romans 8:28 promises—then He is freed from our blind interference in His best-intentioned and perfectly informed purposes for our lives.

How does this translate, practically speaking, into action for our lives? For me at least, this concept is best validated by the past. For instance, when our family was in turmoil over the tumor on Celeste's skull, God was viewing with equal clarity the fact that the hole in her skull would be what would motivate another doctor three years later to take an "optional" CAT scan that would reveal the extensive damage from the invisible skull fracture that if untreated could have taken her life. Even the horror of the tumor experience was something that He very practically used to minimize damage from a yet-future event. And who knows how else He will use these things in our days still to come?

I believe that He will continue to bring blessings out of all these crises I have shared. But even if their "usefulness" in my life has been exhausted, I can say with deep gratitude that God has brought more joy, more peace, more closeness to Himself from out of these events than pain.

But as I said, such things are best assessed when viewed from a time when the crisis is past. How do we in the midst of crisis believe that good can ever come out of the horror we are witnessing?

First of all, we dare not see Him as a purely utilitarian master who "sharpens" us against the whetstones of difficult situations just so he can maximize our effectiveness later. He is, after all, a God with a heart.

And we cannot afford to start constructing "explanations" for what He is doing. Although we can acknowledge results as they become apparent, it is dangerous to try to outguess God's motive in the midst of crisis. A preacher friend of mine, Tim Martin, explained the danger this way. If when we are in trouble, we construct a "chair" for ourselves that has as its legs our own explanations for what God might be doing, such a chair should be regarded as merely ornamental to our minds; for if we rest our weight upon it, we run great risks. If, for instance, one of our explanations turns out to be invalid, we might think, "Well, that's all right, I have three other explanations." Then if a second leg is knocked from under us, we might conclude that the chair can still stand—if we use one of our own legs to stabilize it. If a third leg goes, we might possibly teeter on the single remaining leg and our own two legs to keep the chair operational.

But what happens when our last "explanation" shows itself to be flawed or useless? Our own legs, bent and spasming, show they are not meant to hold up chairs; and we who depend upon chairs of explanations fall.

I mentioned before that I cannot at this time see the "why" of my mother's stroke and Celeste's fall. I do know that living through these events has made me more able to speak with some authority to other Christians about crisis. But I refuse to believe that God inflicted a stroke and a concussion on two people I love for the sole purpose of making me write a better book. If that were so, and you could buy this book for even a fraction of what it cost them and me, you would not dare to price it.

Philip Yancey, in *Where Is God When It Hurts*, dealt with a discomforting fact: there simply are not always explanations for why things happen to believing people or to those they love. Some people suffer tragedy and go to their graves without any tangible proof that their suffering was "for" any purpose at all. (Perhaps equally significant is the fact that such people may be convinced that any lessons learned or growth achieved could have been derived from a less painful teaching method.)

I am grateful to God that He allows us the freedom to at least deal with such feelings and possibilities without striking us dead for thinking such questioning thoughts. Perhaps that is because He knows that those who seek Him, ultimately find Him; and those that find Him discover He is always good, if not always self-explanatory.

We know that He does not owe us explanations for what He is doing or has done, and yet we crave them with an unshakable thirst. We search for answers in our own experiences and those of others, ransack the Scriptures for parallels, rack our brains for constructs. Usually, though, these searches are not completely satisfying and ultimately lead us to the One who has the answers we seek, the changes we feel we must have.

And of course we seek the God who can change things for us. Bookstore shelves are bulging with those books that tell us to just have faith, to "claim" promises we find in the Scriptures, and give us to believe that God is somehow bound in ropes of His own reliability to keep any promise made to anyone else in the Bible if we just decide that it applies to us. (Those who emerge from crises bankrupt or bereaved or brokenhearted are told to conclude that the fault was theirs; next time they should be more faith-filled, pray more, give more . . .)

Of course we correct this kind of thinking with the knowledge that God's promises are often conditional but always fulfilled with the best interests of the individual in mind—a theme we will explore more fully in the next chapter.

But as we sit in the hospital chapel or the ambulance or the anteroom of an office where bad news awaits us, how can we muster up praise? We may be able to tell others around us that God is in control of our situation, but what do we say to Him when we are alone with Him and things are going very, very badly?

It seems to me that the praise we offer Him at such a time is truly sacrificial in that in order to praise we must put aside our inclinations to panic or feel sorry for ourselves or blame God or others for our situation. By a conscious act of will we deliberately dispense with those options and follow the admonition in Philippians 4:6 to not be overcome with anxiety, to ask for what we need, to thank Him in all situations.

No easy task if we consider that the God we are thanking for this unmanageable situation could (theoretically) have prevented it.

What resources allow us to do such unnatural things as be calm, confidently ask, thank? Are we to lay aside our humanness in respect to His requirement of praise?

It is in such times that we suddenly understand what we have "known" all along, that the obvious becomes overwhelming: God doesn't need our praise—we need to praise Him. He doesn't depend upon how we see Him, but we certainly do. The sacrifice of praise becomes not only fire-consumed food offered up to Him but a meal whose greatest part we, like the Levites, share with Him; and as our hunger is satisfied we realize how kind it was of Him to require it of us, how great our privilege to eat the choicest meat in His presence.

And that is exactly what we feed upon in crisis: what we offer to Him is what will sustain us. If it is the lifeless words of others, the catechism of the faith of those around us that we lift to God, then we will be as unsatisfied as He. When it is just God and me in a fear-filled room, usually the praise-phrases of others seem secondhand and unfitted for the task of addressing God, even as reading from a book about praise (even a good book about praise) was unsuitable for the seminar I taught.

No, there are more nourishing sources. One fount of praise that never runs dry even when we are withered within is the bubbling spring of Scripture. I cannot count the times that I have been comforted by the fact that the God I serve is the One who led the Israelites through the Red Sea. If He could hold back an army, harness hydraulics, and assign His attention to each man, woman, child, and animal in that ragtag party, then He can surely help me no matter how bleak my day—for He is God and that is the way He was then, and that is how He is now.

But there is another book, too, whose pages I can recite when all other comfort seems far away.

I can read to Him my history, the recounting of His deeds in my own days, the book of how He has worked in my life that is written on my heart, even when that heart is too broken to record any other epilogue than this:

In my life, He has always been strong. He has always been loving.

I feel the flat cool blade of
Your sword upon my shoulder
As I bow, looking only
At your feet

You, the prince of my heart,
Bequeath it to me

The gift you have given me
Is my own life

NINE
Prayer in Crisis

From the beginning, writing this book has been like raising a child, a headstrong child at that. I originally planned for it to be well-behaved, an example for others.

But as it matured, it proved to have a mind of its own. It has run off into places I never intended it to go. It has opened dark cupboards I had forgotten, and dragged out their contents. Instead of being the reflection of the good qualities I wanted to pass on, it has, like all children, shown its parent to be weak, vulnerable, and prone to mistakes.

As I prepare to send it out into the world, it nags me now, telling me that in the area of prayer, I must leave aside the theories and share openly what I have learned about how God answers prayer, especially in crisis.

But I don't want to do that. I want to repeat for you all the true and valuable things other people have said—people like Andrew Murray and Tim Stafford and Watchman Nee and Richard J. Foster and C. S. Lewis—all of whom have strengthened me immeasurably. I had intended to relate faith-building stories about men like "Praying" Hyde, who prayed so intensely that his heart actually moved to the opposite side of his body, and the story of George Müller, who had a list of unsaved friends he prayed for daily, and how every single one of them eventually became a Christian.

You see, I wanted to share about how to set up a prayer log, and how to use it daily, as I do. I wanted to give you some "jumpstart" hints about how to get started with a consistent, satisfying daily prayer time. I planned to impress upon your mind the importance of meditation before and during daily prayer time.

And then there was the great theory I was going to unveil for the world. I was going to tell about how God is like the One-Minute Manager in that He quickly answers prayers for people who are just beginning to pray and then as we mature, how He suspends answering some prayers; and so we learn patience.

And oh, the funny stories I was going to tell. Some were bittersweet memories of public prayers I've heard. Like the recollection of the man who stood up in front of our congregation and solemnly announced, "Will you pray to me?" and then shut his eyes and led a beautiful prayer. Or the time when services were ending that someone else offered, "Let us close our mind with prayer." And the time that the man who wanted to impress us all with his vocabulary prayed sincerely for our preacher, whom he termed "the orifice of God."

And so I was going to encourage everyone not to use fine-sounding words or trite phrases, but to be open and honest with God in prayer.

The child has nearly jerked my arm off with impatience. All that stuff is either found in other books or (the child reminds me) has nothing to do with crisis. That child has the face of the young widow I talked to about a year ago, telling her about this neat book I was going to write about prayer in crisis; the young woman who told me flatly that finding out how to pray to prepare for crisis was pretty worthless when you were already in the middle of it, and that prayer logs and such do not warm an empty bed or answer her fatherless children's questions.

She was right.

For no matter how much I have emphasized the importance of knowing who God is and what He has done in the past; for all the cautioning that I have done about the urgency of these two things as a basis for the third part of praise, which is confidence in Him to help in present circumstances and to help us understand who we are—in spite of all this, I know that there are those people who will read this right in the middle of the most devastating experiences of their lives who won't be comforted much by the fact that they did not prepare for what they are undergoing.

When the breadwinner of a family dies uninsured, his widow knows that things would have been better if he'd seen fit to buy insurance, but her first thought is getting a job. When our car breaks down, we may nod along with the mechanic who tells us we should have changed the oil more regularly, but what we really want to know is, can it be fixed and if so, how much will it cost?

The principle is the same in crisis. Can it be fixed? How much will it cost? We know that a stable relationship with God would have limited the damage, but now we are just concerned with cutting our losses.

The tools for building a relationship with God sometimes just aren't the right tools for the job of dealing with a crisis. I depend heavily on my daily prayer log, but if you think I went to it while Celeste was in the hospital and prayed carefully for the missionaries and "lost causes" I remember in "normal times," then you don't know me very well.

I had only one "cause" on my mind. What I wanted to know was, Can it be fixed? How much will it cost?

In crisis, we usually face our feelings of impotence and frustration by wanting first of all to pay as many costs as we possibly can ourselves. That is why we make bargains with God, promising that not only will we do whatever is necessary to "cure" the present situation, but often offering also to make sweeping reforms in other areas of our lives that we believe are not pleasing to God.

When we become promisers we must be realistic and acknowledge that it is the crisis, the unmanageable situation we face, that has caused us to be brought to the point of doing something. But still, we want God to do what we think is needed, right now; we want the goods immediately and for Him to take a credit voucher for our future improvements. And why not? Isn't He a strong God? And hasn't our credit been good with Him in the past when we placed orders?

The danger is not in making such promises, it is in thinking that we bind God by so doing. And often, the ultimate cost is higher than we thought, the payment schedule longer than we'd anticipated.

In short, there's nothing wrong with a promise—just so you remember that promises to God have to be made without condition as to what He "must" do in return, and they have to be kept regardless of the ultimate cost. Let's be honest—such a deal more closely resembles a gamble than a negotiation. And we, not God, are always the ones who initiate such.

But after we busywork humans have appeased our consciences by doing all we know to do, then we return to God with the first, urgent question, Can it be fixed?

We make this appeal through prayer. The root of our English word *pray*, in fact, means to ask. Once we have satisfied the praise requirements of knowing and acknowledging we get to the crux of what these things enable us to ask.

The fact of asking presupposes that we believe Someone is listening, Someone who at least has the power to respond to us. We want to lock onto the Being that has in the past stopped rivers and won wars and raised the dead. Ephesians tells us that He is "able to do immeasurably more than all we ask or imagine" (3:20), and in crisis we find ourselves admitting that we'd settle just for what we had in mind, thank you, and forget about all the things beyond our imagining.

We who have been taught all our lives to make our prayers specific so that we can know for a certainty when they have been answered have no trouble with saying, "Save her life" or "Heal my child" or "Stop this pain." We take the assurance of James 4:2, which tells us that we have not because we ask not or because we ask selfishly; we remember that Jesus commanded us to pray and not give up—to ask, knock, seek.

But we look at accident-shattered bodies and disease-ravaged limbs and empty bank accounts and abandoned wives; we wonder if those promises were really for us and even if we have any power to change the mind of God if He has decided to let these things continue.

Yes, He listens. He sent an angel to answer Daniel's prayer from the moment Daniel began to pray (Daniel 9:23). Prayer suspended rain on a country for three and a half years, James 5:17 tells us, assuring us that it was the prayer of "a man just like us."

Prayer is powerful enough to cause the forgiveness of sins, as we see in Job 42:8 and 2 Chronicle 30:17-20. It can part waters, bring down walls, make the sun stand still.

Even Jesus Himself challenged us to believe in what we ask for in prayer, saying in Mark 11:22-24 that with sufficient faith we could cause a mountain to move into a sea. (Talk about questionable motives—what possible good would moving a mountain into the sea do? Think of the tidal waves it would cause, the loss of lives and property.) But this was His lesson, not mine, and He taught it with the specific purpose of getting us to think seriously about the consequences, not just the power, of prayer.

One aspect of the power of prayer that we usually don't talk too much about—but upon which we rely heavily in crisis—is the assumption we make that prayer has an impact on the emotions of God. We take it for granted that God is moved not only by our situations but also by our appeals for help.

In other words, we believe we can "get to" God with our prayers. And we are right in so thinking. The exact representation of God, His Son Jesus, who reflected His nature like a mirror, saw human suffering and responded with compassion—and the Greek wording suggests a physical reaction wherein His intestines knotted up with the intensity of His feeling. Chuck Swindoll, in *For Those Who Hurt*, observed that "a teardrop on earth summons the King of Heaven. Rather than being ashamed or disappointed, the Lord takes note of our inner friction when hard times are oiled by tears."

And it was Jesus Himself who told the parable about a persistent widow who with her constant entreaties was able to "wear down" the resistance of a judge who could make a difference in her situation. Luke informs us that Jesus told this parable with the specific purpose of motivating His disciples to "always pray and not give up" (Luke 18:1).

Another parable on prayer, that of the friend at midnight (Luke 11), is tremendously encouraging to those of us who find ourselves in desperate need and yet know that we are not satisfied in our hearts that our relationship with God entitles us to any special consideration. In this parable, a need is filled not on the basis of the relationship of the giver and the receiver, but because of the urgency of the requirement and the boldness of the asker. This shows us that God does indeed respond to urgent human need and reminds us that our persistence in asking doesn't prove anything to the God who already knows us intimately, but rather proves to us our own sincerity.

Our own desperation *does* mater. Persistent pleading *does* make a difference. If the God of the universe has prayer "hot buttons" then these are they.

And yet we do not want a God we can control, not really. At the mention of such unforeseen power in our prayer, we Christians breathe a sigh of relief and figure, whew, that was a close call but thank goodness there's "Thy will be done" to protect us from such things. We who do not want to take full responsibility for our prayers use this phrase as the escape clause of Christianity, the parachute of prayer.

That's because, I think, we who have suffered crisis have misunderstood submission. Oh, we think we understand submission all too well, we who have been ground under the heel of circumstances we hate, situations that have mastered us and taken on personalities of ruthless taskmasters. But we have made the mistake of thinking it is the disaster that is inevitable, not the will of God. Both are implacable, immovable; but there is a big difference between the two: the situation has no feelings, no love for us. God does.

When we declare our independence from the situation and place ourselves under His dominion, everything changes. Our new Master loves us.

His acceptance of us frees us to dream dreams, to look beyond present circumstances with their now-limited tentacles, and to directly address Him who has the power over both. In prayer, we construct a world that does not exist. We then ask God, who calls things that are not as though they were (Romans 4:17), to make it a reality. We depend upon Him, who sees clearly every single person and every single possible consequence of our prayers, to do what is right and good. If what we have asked for coincides with truth—God's perfect vision of what is best for each individual situation—then He will bring it about. He can do it because He is strong. He wants to do it because He is loving. And even our persistent prayers won't budge Him into doing something eternally harmful to us or anyone else, because He is God.

We sometimes forget that prayer in crisis fills a very profound need for us: that of being able to talk to someone who completely understands our situation and all its ramifications. Even if we were to discount the fact that our Listener has the power to help with the situation, prayer itself has a tremendous cathartic benefit for us.

But prayer Is not just self-oriented. It is more than just therapy.

It seems to me that prayer in crisis usually involves two basic questions that we ask God (variations on the theme of Can it be fixed" and How much will it cost?). They are: First, Why has this happened? And second, What will You do about it?

We have already acknowledged that the first question is one to which we cannot demand an answer. My friend Kay Beaty, who is in the middle of chemotherapy treatments for breast cancer, told me yesterday that she is reserving her question until she can ask God face-to-face in heaven:

"Was this really necessary?" Her query reflects not only her very natural and normal feelings, but also her faith that there will ultimately be an explanation, though it probably won't ever be clear on earth.

Once we, like Kay, have accepted that we probably won't know here the why of our situation, then we are free to make the decision to trust our God—without holding our hearts hostage until He pays the ransom of an explanation.

The second question we ask of God in crisis-prayer is what will He do to change either us or the situation we are in. I find myself at this point forced to say something so obvious that it is almost tiresome, but so necessary as to be obligatory.

No one can foresee the future. I cannot, nor can anyone, tell you if God will do for you what you are so urgently asking Him to do. And whatever it is He will do, you probably don't really want to know ahead of time.

There are so many times that I have prayed to know the will of God for specific situations and found that I received no answer I could identify as such. I have wondered if there was something else in myself that I needed to change in order to aid His bringing about fulfillment of my request. (You know the script: "just tell me, Lord—what do you want from me? I will do whatever you say, just make the hurting stop. . . ")

In the end, though, I have concluded that, after we have done all we know to do to facilitate His actions, sometimes God's unexplained timing must prevail.

Am I saying that praying doesn't really matter, that God is "gonna do what He's gonna do"?

Quite the contrary. The inherently good God we serve lets us, through prayer, participate in bringing about good things. Pascal said that He allows us the dignity of being the "causes" of His actions. Tim Stafford, in *Knowing the Face of God*, goes a step further: "God's decision to wait for our prayers is his second humiliation to the flesh. In the first, he stripped off his glory and became a man to destroy the forces keeping God and man apart. Now he holds his power in check and waits for us to care."

The release of this great power is what we interpret as answers to our prayers. There are three types of answers to prayers of crisis that I have observed.

The first is the gift of insight. The promise of James 1:5 is as open-ended as any promise in Scripture. What it says is that the hand that reaches out to God for wisdom will never be slapped.

Practically speaking, how is such wisdom conveyed? No Christian can discount the prerogative of God to communicate directly with a believer, even today. (But, as Tim Stafford reminds us, such a communique would have a high price tag: "If we get this kind of a message, we had better obey.") More commonly, wisdom and guidance from God come from an impression on the mind when the Holy Spirit, in response to our prayer for wisdom, lets us see something about ourselves or our situation clearly for the first time.

Another avenue of this wisdom can come in the form of advice from godly advisors, either friends or professional counselors. Sometimes they offer words of wisdom; just as often they serve as conduits for God's love when we are hurting. An example of this love is my friend Sandy Oglesby who flew to Boulder the day after Celeste's tumor surgery. She was the one who "took over" when my knees gave way at the first unwrapping of the wound's dressing. (If you have ever seen a fresh surgical incision, you will understand.)

But sometimes we who listen carefully for God's encouragement are too proud to accept it when it is carried by human hands or lips. I, for instance, was so prideful and self-sufficient that I sent away all my Christian friends from the hospital the first night of my mother's stroke. Had the efforts to resuscitate her when her heart stopped the second time not been successful, I would have been all alone in that hospital.

We were not meant to handle such things alone; like the child afraid of the dark whose mother assured him that his angel was there, we protest, "But I need someone with skin on."

The third and most unimpeachable source of wisdom is of course Scripture, and it should be our primary font. It stands impervious to the fading flowers and grasses of time, circumstances, feelings, and manipulation. Our minds can deceive us, friends can be mistaken or even have unhealthy motives for what they say to us. But Scripture, praise God, has no such failings.

Closely related to the "answer" of wisdom is God's response to prayer that manifests itself in a change in ourselves. Perhaps this has always been for me the most important thing in crisis: it was not as necessary for me to understand a situation as it was to receive the ability from God to handle it as a Christian should. I freely acknowledge that every scrap of courage and resolution and calmness I have felt in crisis was a free gift from God, and not of myself.

Some of my experiences remind me of the massive fires that ravaged Yellowstone National Forest; these experiences left behind charred, blackened places in my heart. It has only been with time that I can see the fresh, new growth within that has enabled me to acknowledge twin truths: I can never go back to the forests of the past, and the forest of my future must rise from those ashes.

Perhaps you too have met people who have never faced a major crisis, while others have faced many. Perhaps we of the second group are like the lodgepole pine, a species of evergreen that covers millions of acres of the northern Rocky Mountains, including Yellowstone. The lodgepole pine, unlike its neighbor trees, can only reproduce after a fire because it relies on heat to open its cones and release the seeds.

Botanists tell us that even if the seeds were released, by, say, cracking open the cones, their seedlings would die without the mineral soil that a fire exposes. As I look around me at loved ones who have been seared by the fires of crisis we have shared, I remember my urgent prayer when I began my spiritual journey distant years ago, a prayer that God would do whatever was necessary to bring me close to Him; and I see that day in the distant past only dimly through the smoke of my days, a haze that yet lingers.

The third type of answer from God to a prayer in crisis is the most obvious: a change in the circumstances of the situation about which we are praying. It is the healing we feel is necessary, the averting of a seemingly inevitable disaster. Because such an answer can be more objectively assessed (than say, the subjective experience of receiving insight, or perceiving that you are being enabled to bear up under bad times), it often carries with it a "divine stamp of approval" in our minds. Because it is so unmistakable, we crave tangible change—results—much like the Jews of Jesus' day, as a sign that we can hang our faith upon.

Of course we see the danger there. If our faith is hanging on a peg of circumstances, it will fall when the circumstances change again, as circumstances usually do. If my faith in God, for example, had been based on Celeste's healing from her skull tumor, then it would have been devastated when that same skull was shattered against a brick wall almost three years later.

Now, I believe, I have almost satisfied the demands of the anxious child this book has become. As much for myself as for anyone else, I will reprise the themes of praise and prayer:

God, who is loving and kind and able to do anything He pleases, listens carefully to the prayers of people in crisis. He does not use such situations of our weakness to take advantage of us or to punish us. He limits the bad effects of any disaster on us, so that no matter what happens we can be assured that without His intervention, things would have been much worse.

His answers to our prayers come in many forms, but often in forms we do not expect. Each answer is a manifestation of His love and power.

He stands ready to give us wisdom and strength in direct proportion to our willingness and desire to receive these two commodities. Those things we understand, we can thank Him for. Those things we cannot understand we must see as evidence of the fact that He Himself cannot be understood by our human minds. All He asks in this case is that we trust Him, because He has the best interests of each person in mind.

He cares. He is perceptibly moved by our pain, in fact, to the point of actually sharing our grief with us.

I am sure of this, as sure as of any other thing in my life. Many times, in uncontrollable circumstances, I, like many others who have suffered, have wept so much that hunger has disappeared. The psalmists—in Psalms 42:3, 80:5, and 102:9—spoke of such grief at times that tears became their food and drink; and I have feasted with them.

But there is Someone else who shares this with us. In Revelation 3:20, Jesus pictured Himself as a guest who waits outside the door of our hearts, asking to come in.

He is the gentle God who won't break the bruised reed of your heart, nor extinguish your dim, flickering wick. He has come to share our lives, good times and bad.

He has come, the Scripture says, to eat with us.

Listen, child of crisis. If the only food we have is our own tears, then He too partakes.

Oh yes . . .

My Jesus cares.

What was, before you,
Was formless and void

My eyes were unable to see
Until you came
And just your touch
Has healed me

And how I treasure the
Living memory
That the first thing
My newly healed eyes saw
Was your lovely face

The Balm
("I have wounded, and I will heal . . . ")

You have wounded
And only you can heal
That breach

The salve is that
Of your honeyed voice

The wine and oil are those
Of your presence

You paid long ago
In advance
For my healing

And so now
No word can hurt me
Nothing can injure me
Without the binding force of
My love for you
Smoothing away the
Edges of a scar
That will never form

My words stand before me
Empty-handed and mute;
They are paupered,
Impotent, helpless.

They are dulled tools,
Blunted blades,
Worn-out carriers
Unequal to their task.

They cannot measure the honey of your words
Cannot weigh out the heaviness of my heart
Cannot wrap around this limitless hope.

But this I know:

When I hear your voice
My heart is made glad

Afterword

Between the time that the writing of this book was completed and the time of publication, I underwent major surgery. I appreciated of the concern shown to me during that time by family and friends and the servant-hearted women of the Mountainside Church of Christ, who cooked my meals for weeks, cleaned my house, watched my children and taxied them to violin lessons and basketball practice, washed my laundry, and prayed for me. A star-in-the-crown award went to Barbara Shannon, who encouraged me on a daily basis, using her past experiences in just the way that the Bible says (2 Corinthians 1:3-4).

In the thirty years that have passed since this book first appeared, our family has added many unwelcome medical terms to our vocabulary: cancers, full-body welt, open heart surgery, pulmonary embolism, necrotizing pancreatitis, septic shock, Epstein-Barr, Cdiff and VRE; and coma and quadriplegia in three variants of Guillain-Barre Syndrome. We have lost my dear mother to death but she lost nothing in the process—she transitioned quickly and peacefully at last to the arms of her Savior.

I praise the God of history ever the more for His strength, which has as always been most perfected in my own weakness.

Additional Notes

Perhaps some readers might like additional scriptural confirmation of certain statements I made. The following are offered with an admonition to use these and all other scriptural quotations wisely and in the sense that their context requires.

Introduction

Insights: Ephesians 1:7-8, Philippians 1:9-10, Colossians 1:9

How Job was answered: Job chapter 38. especially verses 2-3

Life eternal is knowing God: John 17:3

Stephen's recounting of Jewish history: Acts chapter 7

Mary's praise: Luke 1:46-55

Hannah's praise: I Samuel 2:1-10

Solomon's temple dedication prayer: 2 Chronicles 6, especially verses 14-15

Praise of the elders and four living creatures: Revelation 4:8-12

Chapter One

The results of sin: Romans 5:12

Satan: John 8:44

Chapter Three

The Lord's Prayer: Matthew: 6:9-13

God's omniscience: Matthew 6:25-34

God's care for the individual: Matthew 10:29-31

God's foreknowledge of the individual: Jeremiah 1:5

The wood that was worshiped and burned: Isaiah 44:14-20

John's reaction to the Lord: Revelation 1:12-18

Isaiah's reaction to the Lord: Isaiah 6:1-5

Ezekiel's reaction to the Lord: Ezekiel 1:26-28

God paid for us with HIS Son's blood: I Peter 1:17-19

Isaiah passages about the uniqueness of God: 43: 10-1 1; 44:6, 8; 45:5, 21; 46:9

Jesus's eternal, uncreated nature: John 1:1

The Holy Spirit indwells and helps individuals: 2 Timothy 1:14; Romans 8:26-27

Chapter Four

An example of a Scripture writer who was not an eyewitness to what he reported: Luke 1:1-4

God doesn't change: Malachi 3:6; James 1:17

Doing one's duty isn't meritorious: Luke 17:10

David's worship after the death of his infant: 2 Samuel 12: 19-20

Chapter Five

Sabbath rest for land recouped: Leviticus 25:1-7; 26:33-35

Every knee will bow and every tongue confess: Romans 14:1 1; Philippians 2:10-11

We are heirs with Christ: Romans 8:15-17

A few "mighty hand and outstretched arm" passages: Psalm 77:10-12; Deuteronomy 4:34; 11:2; I Kings 8:42; 2 Chronicles 6:32; Psalm 136:12

"What is that in your hand?": Exodus 4:2

Paul and Silas singing in jail: Acts 16:25

Chapter Eight

God is not like man: Isaiah 55:8-9; I Samuel 15:29

Sin came through Adam; its wages is death: Romans 5:12-14, 6:23

God dwells in eternity: Daniel 4:34

"A God with a heart": Psalm 103:13

God will be found by those who seek Him: Jeremiah 29:11-14

Chapter Nine

Importance of keeping a vow to God: Deuteronomy 23:21-23

God is moved by our prayers and responds to us: Daniel 9:21-23;

Isaiah 38:1-5; 63:9; 65:24

Jesus' response of compassion: Matthew 9:36; 14:14; 15:32; 20:34; Mark 1:41; Luke 15:20; James 5:11

The impressions of the Holy Spirit on our minds: Luke 21:15; John 16:5- 15; Ephesians 1:17-18; Philippians 1:9-10; Colossians 1:9

God's gentleness: Isaiah 42:3

For Further Reading in the Bible

The following praise passages are included for further study. Some are addressed to God; others are about God. They show the pattern of praise that I have earlier identified: saying who God is, telling about what He has done in the past, and assessing from these either what He can do in the future or what we should do in response to these facts about God (as in many of the psalms); the response to the first two is the conclusion that we should praise. Sometimes the order of these three elements is switched (see Exodus 15:1—18).

Some end in a negative assessment of what God will do to the wicked instead of the usual positive assessment of what we expect Him to do for the just (see Psalm 95). There is even an example of Jesus Himself praising (Matthew 11:25-27).

Though these passages are in order according to their placement in Bible books, this does not presume to be a comprehensive list. It is my prayer that you will discover some on your own too.

Exodus 15:1-18
Deuteronomy 4:32-40; 32: 1-43
I Samuel 2:1-10
2 Samuel chapter 22
I Kings 8:23-26
1 Chronicles 16:7-36; 29:10-20
2 Chronicles 6:14-17; 20:6-12
Nehemiah 9:5-37
Most of the Psalms, but especially 8, 18, 30, 31, 33, 34, 46, 48, 66, 71, 80, 81, 89, 90, 92, 95, 96, 97, 98, 99, 103, 104, 105, 106, 107, 111, 113, 116, 118, 135, 136, 138, 139, 144, 145, 146, 147, 148, 149, 150.
Isaiah chapters 12, 25, 26

Isaiah 37:15-20; 63:7; 64:12

Jeremiah 32:17-23

Lamentations 3:21-26

Daniel 2:20-23; 3:28-29; 6:26-27

Micah 7:18-20

Nahum 1:2-8

Habakkuk chapter 3

Luke 1:46-55; 67-79

John 17:1-5

Acts 4:24-30; 17:22-31

Romans 11:33-36

2 Corinthians 1:3-7

Ephesians 1:3-23

Philippians 2:6-11

1 Peter 1:3-16

Revelation 4:8, 11; 5:9-10; 7:10-12; 11:15-18; 15:3-4; 16:5-7; 19:1-8

Suggested Books for Further Reading

Here is a list of books that influenced my spiritual development in the areas that this book covered.

Celebration of Discipline by Richard Foster

"Divine Etiquette" by Altne Edson (article in November 1985 *Image* magazine)

For Those Who Hurt by Charles Swindoll

A Grief Observed by C. S. Lewis

The Hallelujah Factor by Jack Taylor

The Hiding Place by Corrie ten Boom

How to Read the Bible for All It's Worth by Gordon D. Fee and Douglas Stuart

Knowing the Face of God by Tim Stafford

The Knowledge of the Holy by A. W. Tozer

Praise: A Doorway to God's Presence by Warren and Ruth Meyers

Time and Eternity by Arthur C. Custance

What Happens When Women Pray by Evelyn Christenson

Where Is God When It Hurts? by Philip Yancey

CPSIA information can be obtained
at www.ICGtesting.com
Printed in the USA
BVHW030556211220
596157BV00001B/14